Evangelization and Culture

Evangelization and Culture

Aylward Shorter

GEOFFREY
CHAPMAN

Geoffrey Chapman
A Cassell imprint
Villiers House, 41/47 Strand, London WC2N 5JE
387 Park Avenue South, New York, NY 10016–8810

First published 1994

British Library Cataloguing-in-Publication Data
A catalogue record for this book is available from the British Library.

Library of Congress Cataloging-in-Publication Data
Applied for.

ISBN 0–225–66723–1

Phototypeset by Intype, London
Printed and bound in Great Britain by
Biddles Ltd, Guildford and King's Lynn

Contents

Note

Biblical quotations are from RSV and the Bible Society's *Chain Reference Bible*, Good News Edition (Swindon, 1985).

Vatican II texts are taken from *Documents on Vatican Council II*, ed. Austin Flannery OP (Dublin: Dominican Publications 1975).

Quotations from papal encyclicals and synodal documents are from editions published by the Catholic Truth Society, London, except for *Redemptoris Missio*, where F. J. McCarthy's more accurate translation in *Millhilliana*, no. 2 (1991) has been used.

Introduction

It has been calculated that there have been 788 global plans to evangelize the world since the beginning of Christianity.[1] So there is nothing new about a Decade of Evangelization to close the second millennium of the Christian era. Most of us are not expecting that the world will suddenly find itself Christian on 1 January 2000. However, the Decade may still be a useful reminder to us to take evangelization more seriously. Evangelization is, after all, the basic commitment of the Church at all times. A Decade of Evangelization may serve as an incentive or stimulus to carry out this commitment more responsibly.

In 1975 Pope Paul VI pointed out that evangelization is addressed to culture, as part of the human phenomenon.[2] This insight has contributed to the development of the idea of inculturation, or the dialogue between faith and culture, as an indispensable aspect of evangelization. In 1988 I published an attempt to summarize the thinking of the Catholic Church on the subject of inculturation.[3] In the light of this book, I was invited to deliver the Albert Cardinal Meyer Lectures at St Mary of the Lake University, Mundelein, Chicago in April 1991, on the subject of 'Inculturation to World Church – the Legacy of Vatican Two'. I set about reading all that had been published on inculturation in the three years since my book appeared, and I found a remarkable consensus among theologians and canonists that inculturation was ultimately an ecclesiological problem.

In the present book, I have argued that, if the evangelization of culture is to be taken seriously, it must lead to the model of a culturally polycentric Church, and to a paradigm of mission which is no longer centred on Europe. It must also lead to a 'new evangelization', that is to say, an evangelization which does not dominate or alienate others culturally, as happened frequently in the history of the Church, but one which loves and respects others in their difference. Chapter 1 studies the nature of evangelization and the interrelationship of Christ, Church and Kingdom. Chapter

2 examines the integral elements of evangelization: dialogue, inculturation and liberation. Chapter 3 looks at evangelization from the point of view of the triple vocation, contemplative, pastoral and missionary. Chapter 4 enumerates the obstacles to evangelization that are found both within and outside the Church. The last two chapters consider the model of Church required for effective evangelization, with particular reference to the basic ecclesial community.

Much of Chapters 2, 4 and 5 has been taken from the, as yet, unpublished Albert Cardinal Meyer Lectures. These chapters also owe something to a paper I gave in 1991 to a colloquium at Louvain in honour of the late Professor Frank De Graeve, (published in Louvain Theological and Pastoral Monographs, no. 9).[4] Parts of Chapters 2 and 4 also appeared in a book published in Nairobi in 1991.[5]

On 9 November 1990 I was invited to deliver a paper entitled 'The Vision of Evangelization Offered by the Developing Churches' to a pastoral consultation of Westminster Archdiocese at London Colney. The consultation was on 'Formation for Evangelization'. Subsequently, in 1991, I was asked to speak on evangelization at Milton Keynes, Damascus House, the London Irish Chaplaincy and St Patrick's Soho Square. In all these places a stimulating discussion helped me to formulate and develop the ideas about evangelization to be found in this book. I am also indebted to colleagues and students at the Missionary Institute London where many of these ideas have been aired and shared.

Finally, three cautions must be given. Firstly, the author is a Roman Catholic priest, and this book is basically written with a Roman Catholic outlook. Secondly, the author is also an African missionary, and this accounts for the African interest of the book. Thirdly, the terminology: 'evangelization', 'evangelism', 'mission', 'witness' and so forth, is slippery. Many different shades of meaning are given to these terms. I have tried to give them precise meanings of my own. These may not coincide with the meanings ascribed to them by other authors, but I believe that they help to clarify the discussion, and that they are sufficiently commonplace to be acceptable.

Aylward Shorter
The Missionary Institute London
August 1993

References

1 David Bosch, *Transforming Mission* (Maryknoll, NY: Orbis Books, 1991), p. 419, quoting David B. Barrett and James W. Reapsome, *Seven Hundred Plans to Evangelize the World: The Rise of a Global Evangelization Movement* (Birmingham: New Hope, 1988).
2 Paul VI, *Evangelii Nuntiandi*, 20.
3 Aylward Shorter, *Toward a Theology of Inculturation* (London: Geoffrey Chapman/Maryknoll, NY: Orbis Books, 1988).
4 Aylward Shorter, 'Inculturation, the Premise of Universality' in Catherine Cornille and Valeer Neeckebrouck (eds), *A Universal Faith? – Peoples, Cultures, Religions and the Christ* (Louvain Theological and Pastoral Monographs 9; Louvain, 1992), pp. 1–19.
5 Aylward Shorter, *The African Synod: A Personal Response to the Outline Document* (Nairobi: St Paul Publications Africa, 1991), ch. 6.

*For graduates and students
of the Missionary Institute London*

1 Evangelization and the Kingdom

Christian evangelization and the 'Christ factor'

'Christianity and African Culture': the topic was calculated to draw a large crowd of academics, students and internationals, and the organizers were not disappointed. The élite of Nairobi was there, thronging the brightly lit conference hall in the city centre. A distinguished panel of Kenyan speakers took their place on the platform: a playwright who was also a professor of literature, a popular novelist, a Christian minister who was also a university lecturer in religious studies. With them was a white missionary, feeling nervous and a little out of place. The missionary was billed to speak first, no doubt in order to be shot down afterwards by the 'home team'. His brief was to tell the audience how far the Christian Church could go in the direction of Africanization. What was there in Christianity which could not be given up or changed?

The missionary rose and spoke for half an hour. By and large he endorsed the idea of an African reinterpretation of the Gospel, but he pointed out that Jesus Christ was a historical person and that the Church was a historical institution. There was, he said, a track of meaning that went back to the texts of the Bible and the historical contexts in which the Bible was read and understood. This could not be denied or contradicted.

The two African writers were not theologians, and when called upon to speak did not take serious issue with the missionary. It was left to the minister to respond to what the missionary had said. He rose with great solemnity, and in ringing tones pronounced the words: 'There will never be an African Christianity until we eliminate the Christ factor!'

Probably no one remembered much else of what the last speaker said. It sounded so daring and controversial. But did it make sense? On the face of things, it was a plea for a Christianity without Christ, an appeal to Christians to take seriously the traditional

1

religions of Africa as catering for all the religious needs of African believers, without the need for missionaries. Ultimately, it was an emphatic denial of the need for Christian evangelization. We are familiar with the endless stream of books by secular humanists and free-thinking writers, who want a 'user-friendly' Gospel and a Jesus they can believe in, with the supernatural edited out, but this was a Christianity without any Christ at all, even the most painless and anodyne.

Nonetheless, the speaker seemed to profess an allegiance to Christianity in some form. It was, perhaps, an anonymous, invisible Christianity, a Christianity which could be deduced from the religious experience of Africa, without recourse to a culturally and racially unacceptable prophet of another age, race and country. It was, to use Efoé-Julien Pénoukou's colourful phrase, an instance of 'theological apartheid'. It was an assertion of auto-salvation, comparable in some ways to the secular theologian insisting that human salvation requires no external intervention from God.[1] No doubt, it was also a blow struck against the universalist claims of Christianity. In certain academic circles, what is called the 'uniqueness' of Christ has been widely questioned, although it should be a disservice to religious faith to question the uniqueness of any religion.[2]

There may have been, in the minister's declaration, an implicit reference to the idea of a 'Kingdom of God' which transcends the narrow concept of 'Christianity' or 'Church'. The idea of the 'servant Church', the Church at the service of the Kingdom or the world, is well known, but there are some who emphasize the Kingdom at the expense of Church. In their view, either Church implantation is unnecessary, or the Church is called upon to 'die', so that the world might live.[3] Other writers have called upon Christian neophytes in newly evangelized cultures to reinvent the Church, without reference to the existing local Churches which evangelized them, or to a worldwide communion of local Churches.[4] However, it is one thing to envisage the emergence of faith communities, rather than to emphasize the institutional character of the Church, but it is quite another to abandon the idea of Church or Church communion altogether.[5]

The speaker was clearly anxious to place African traditional religion on a par with Christianity. So it was also obvious that, for him, Christianity offered a norm or standard by which to measure the respectability and salvific potential of other religions. He wanted his religious tradition to be recognized as 'Christianity', but without reference – even anonymous reference – to the person of Christ. The 'Christ factor' must go.

The most obvious rejoinder to such a statement is that 'Christness' depends on Christ, and that 'Christianity' has no meaning if it rejects any reference to him. Jesus did not bequeath a set of teachings to his followers, a message that was called 'Christianity'. Jesus himself is the Good News. His teaching is centred – almost scandalously – on himself. 'Who do you say that I am?'; 'I am the Way, the Truth and the Life'; 'I am the Vine'; 'I am the Bread of Life'; 'I am the Good Shepherd'. Jesus himself is what the Gospel offers to the world, the subject of his own message. As Edward Schillebeeckx remarked: 'Christianity is not the religion of a book, but of a person'.[6] For a Christian, the act of faith is not merely notional assent to a number of dogmas or doctrines. It is a living and transforming encounter with the risen Christ, a union with him which is distinguished by all the characteristics of a relationship of mutual love and trust. It is a relationship nourished by the sacraments, and by a communion with God-in-Christ through prayer – a worshipping relationship, therefore. The risen Christ is everywhere present, and his Spirit of love is everywhere at work. He is waiting, in his turn, to be recognized, loved, invoked. Christian faith opens the believer's eyes to this powerful omnipresence and makes him or her a channel of Christ's love.

In the Gospels we do not only find words attributed to Jesus. He proclaims who and what he is through the reported actions of his life. Moreover, there is no hiatus or discontinuity between the earthly Jesus and the Christ of post-resurrection faith. The passion and death of Jesus are a recapitulation of his life, and the apostles know that the presence of the risen Christ is rooted in an earthly life that really has been lived. Moreover, it is the passion, death and resurrection of Christ which empower the believer to share in his healing and saving mission. All of these reflections indicate that the experience of Christ is essential to Christianity. Even more important is the understanding of the apostles that Jesus Christ did not just show them what God was like, but that, in him, they actually had an experience of God. It was this experience that led the Johannine communities to formulate Christ's divinity in uncompromising terms, to declare their faith that the pre-existing Word of God had become incarnate in Jesus Christ, and that this Word was no ideal personification, but a real divine person 'made flesh' (John 1:14).

All of this proves that it is nonsense to speak of 'Christianity without the Christ factor'. It also demonstrates that the 'Christness' of other faiths and religious traditions, as well as of Christianity itself, ultimately depends on the power and influence – explicit and implicit – of the risen Christ. Fundamentally, it depends on the action of his Holy Spirit. The evident contradiction contained in the Kenyan minister's declaration, however, may serve as a useful starting-point for a discussion of all that is implied by Christian evangelization. It raises all the issues: Kingdom, Church, dialogue, inculturation and liberation. It is with these causes and consequences of evangelization – and the nature of evangelization itself – that this book is concerned.

Evangelization, evangelism: what's in a name?

Roman Catholics speak about 'evangelization', but many Protestants prefer 'evangelism'.[7] We hear a great deal about the Decade of Evangelization or of Evangelism, as the case may be – a ten-year period of extra effort on the part of Christians to communicate their faith, in the run-up to the start of the third millennium. Whatever term is used, the idea underlying it is that the Christian faith has to be shared by means of an active apostolate. The spreading and deepening of the Christian faith depends upon such faith-sharing. People are not converted to Christ by spontaneous personal reflection or introspection, but by hearing the Good News of Jesus Christ from an evangelizer. In other words, it is the result of an interpersonal, even an intercultural, process. The spreading of this Good News is a reconciling activity that brings individuals, communities and nations together. Christians are conscious that this is willed by Christ. Indeed, the so-called 'great commission' at the end of the Synoptic Gospels explicitly envisages such a process of sharing: 'Go, make disciples of every nation' (Matt 28:19; Mark 16:15; Luke 24:47). For the same reason, Christians are conscious of the Good News being of universal significance to all humanity. It is for 'every creature', for 'the whole world', for 'all nations'. These assumptions will be examined later in this book, but it is to be noted that they are integral to the Christian understanding of evangelization or evangelism.

The words 'evangelization' and 'evangelism' derive from the Greek term *evangelion*, meaning the 'good news'. An old English form of the term is *godspell*, from which our modern word 'Gospel' derives. It also means 'good message' or 'good news'. The idea of 'good news' goes back to the tradition of Isaiah and the Psalms. It refers to the messianic good news, the glad tidings that God's universal reign has begun:

> How beautiful upon the mountains
>   are the feet of him who brings good tidings,
> who publishes peace, who brings good tidings of good,
>   who publishes salvation,
>   who says to Zion, 'Your God reigns.' (Isaiah 52:7)

4

We find a similar proclamation of God's final reign over humanity in Psalm 96. This good news is about God's favour towards those who mourn, who are afflicted, broken-hearted, captive and in prison. It is a promise of comfort, encouragement and liberation. In Third Isaiah the good news is described in just those terms (Isaiah 61:1–3). Jesus also preached God's Kingdom in these terms, and spent his public life among the sick, the afflicted and the outcasts. Luke describes the scene in the synagogue at Nazareth in which Jesus applied Isaiah's idea of good news to his own Gospel.

> And he came to Nazareth where he had been brought up; and he went to the synagogue, as his custom was, on the sabbath day. And he stood up to read; and there was given to him the book of the prophet Isaiah. He opened the book and found the place where it was written,
>
> > 'The Spirit of the Lord is upon me,
> > because he has anointed me to preach the good news to the poor.
> >
> > He has sent me to proclaim release to the captives,
> > and recovering of sight to the blind
> > to set at liberty those who are oppressed,
> > to proclaim the acceptable year of the Lord.'
>
> And he closed the book, and gave it back to the attendant, and sat down; and the eyes of all in the synagogue were fixed upon him. And he began to say to them, 'Today this scripture is fulfilled in your hearing'. (Luke 4:16–21)

This Christian Gospel is therefore the Good News of Jesus Christ, the fulfilment of the promised Kingdom. In a secondary and derived sense, four books of the New Testament are called 'gospels', but the word fundamentally applies to the Christ event.

To 'evangelize' or to 'gospelize' is to make known the Good News of Jesus Christ. The word 'evangelism' is used by some members of Reformation Churches to denote an emphasis on verbal proclamation, on preaching and teaching, even a reliance on verbalistic preaching alone to win the world for Christ and hasten the day of his second coming. The word is associated with great public rallies, like those of Dr Billy Graham and other evangelists. It may express a concern to reach as many people as possible by the most efficient means of communication. The word 'evangelical' refers to those Churches or contexts in which an emphasis is placed on personal conversion in response to the proclaimed word, a conversion based on faith in the atonement through the death of Jesus Christ. Generally speaking, it may be said that the words 'evangelism' and 'evangelical' indicate that a priority is given to verbal proclamation, although the whole mission of the Church is not always identified with evangelism.

This is a characteristic emphasis in the Decade of Evangelization/Evangelism. Proclamation is seen as the 'first duty' of evangelization and the end to which all evangelistic activity is directed.[8] No doubt, there is a widespread reticence on the part of ordinary Christians to speak openly about their faith, and the emphasis on verbal proclamation is a timely corrective. There are many reasons for this reticence. One is the difficulty we have in speaking about intimate religious experience to outsiders. Another is reluctance to draw attention to oneself. However, the most fundamental reason is that, in a secular and pluralistic world, all religion, and especially Christianity, has been privatized. In the Western, technological culture, religion is thought not to belong to the public domain, but to be a purely private concern. People are embarrassed to parade their religious convictions, and feel threatened by other religious traditions.

There are certainly grounds for this fear and embarrassment. The announcement of the Decade of Evangelization/Evangelism has been greeted with dismay by the adherents of several non-Christian faiths. Jews and Muslims, in particular, have felt that a campaign was being directed against them, and certain crude forms of Christian proselytism have lent weight to their suspicions. Atheists and agnostics have also felt that this was a new and unwelcome form of Christian militancy. When Christians organize 'missions' and 'crusades', or talk of harnessing the electronic media for evangelism, and when evangelistic agencies plot the numerical growth of Christian denominations, people feel that they are being unfairly targeted. A 'foot-in-the-door' style of evangelism is rightly regarded as a nuisance. Evangelism, however, is very far from being a form of proselytism, and, as we shall see, demands extreme sensitivity towards the convictions of non-Christian believers and unbelievers. It demands, in fact, a commitment to genuine dialogue.

There are also reasons connected with the spread of the Gospel itself which suggest that over-emphasis on the priority of verbal proclamation is misplaced. The great commission, 'Go teach all nations', must be balanced by the great commandment, 'Love one another, just as I have loved you' (John 15:11). The commandment to love originates in God's love, embodied in Jesus Christ, and it is even more fundamental, as a source of evangelization, than the commission to teach. This is not to say that proclamation can be dispensed with, or that explicit reference to Jesus Christ is unnecessary. Practical love needs to be informed and critically controlled by faith. The point at issue is really the form which proclamation takes, and the correct circumstances in which it is to be made. 'The hungry man has no ears', says an African proverb. One cannot expect someone who is starving, or numbed by pain, for example, to be convinced by verbal argument. One must first attend to his or her bodily needs before the argument can appear cogent. This is common sense, but it is also an imperative of the Gospel to feed the hungry and minister to the suffering. The world does not easily forgive the religious hypocrite who preaches, but does not practise, a Gospel of universal love.

This was the point of view of Jesus Christ. Again and again, the gospels report him denouncing those who pay lip-service, those whose actions belie their words. The Word of God is not something merely to be spoken or heard; it has to be carried out in practice. Some of Jesus' harshest criticisms were reserved for those he regarded as hypocrites. 'Beware of the yeast of the Pharisees, that is their hypocrisy' (Luke 12:1). 'Woe to you scribes and Pharisees, hypocrites!' (Matt 23:13–27).

Verbal proclamation is not the only form of communication among human beings. There are numerous methods of non-verbal communication, particularly through images and signs. In fact, since religions are by sociological definition symbol-systems, and since the act of faith is essentially an imaginative act, it is not surprising that visual images sometimes have a greater impact on people than purely verbal statements. As J. H. Newman pointed out, merely notional assent is insufficient to produce conviction. What is required is real or imaginative assent.

A recent survey, conducted by the ecumenical body Churches Together in England, demonstrated that verbal preaching plays little part in religious conversion. Big evangelistic rallies and mission gatherings are the least effective means of spreading the Gospel and of bringing people to faith in Christ.[9] Their influence is at best transitory and superficial. What affects people and brings about religious conversion in most cases is a relationship of love: friendship, courtship, marriage. Again, this is entirely in line with the nature of the Gospel itself, which is essentially a revelation of divine love. The people most likely to accept the Gospel message from us are those whom we genuinely and unreservedly love.

Since the term 'evangelism' sometimes tends to denote an undue emphasis on verbal proclamation, it is probably preferable to use the term 'evangelization'. This will be the usage of this book. Evangelization is a more comprehensive term. It suggests that the process is considerably more than one of verbal teaching and preaching alone. The Word must not only be proclaimed: it must also be celebrated and lived. We should get away from all mechan-

7

istic images of communication, and concentrate on the concept of experiential communion, of sharing. More will be said later in this book about the place of the mass media in evangelization. Too great an emphasis on verbal proclamation may entail the risk of over-reliance on the media, and of manipulation by the media. Effective evangelization takes place through first-hand experience and action, rather than through teaching and theory alone. A basic slogan of this book, therefore, is that evangelization comprises proclamation, praxis and prayer.

The Good News of the Kingdom

Evangelization is the spreading of the Good News about God's Kingdom and the realization of the Kingdom. 'Kingdom' is the word that Jesus used, and he lived in a time when kingship was the ordinary form taken by political authority. The concept of 'king', or indeed 'queen', varies from one cultural tradition to another. In some cases, the king was also a god, or the reincarnation of a semi-divine ancestor. In other traditions, he was a ritual agent with a cosmic role, a 'tabooed' individual, a divine king who guaranteed the prosperity and harmony of his people, and was perhaps even a cosmic sacrifice for his people. Ideas of kingship are somewhat attenuated in the twentieth century, but the concept which underlies all these royal manifestations is that of the sacred person, the monarch who rules by divine permission and sanction. When Jesus used the term 'king', we can be sure that this sacred character was an important part of his understanding of the term.

Having said that, we immediately notice that Jesus went to great lengths to stress the difference between God's Kingdom and the royal institutions of his time. The Kingdom is 'not of this world'. It is 'within' or 'among' you, and exists for those 'who belong to the truth', those who are humble and who become like little children, the 'little ones' (Luke 17:21; John 18:37–38; Matt 18:4). It is clear, therefore, that spreading the Good News of this Kingdom can have nothing remotely to do with conquest, spiritual, cultural or military. It is not a message that is imposed by force. Jesus did not make himself the leader of a nationalist uprising, as some of his followers hoped.

During the fifth centenary of Christopher Columbus's voyage to the Americas, we were reminded many times that Christian evangelization was largely a concomitant of military conquest in that continent. Whether it was effected by the Spanish or Portuguese conquistadors, or by militant settlers from Protestant northern Europe, force was used against the aboriginal American peoples. The same must be said of the evangelization of Africa, Asia and Oceania, which largely took place at the moment of nineteenth-century European colonial expansion. Although links between missionary and colonist were often complex and subtle, European technological, military and economic superiority weighed strongly with tribal peoples who usually made no distinction between Church and State, or between religion and politics. The Christian Church is still identified in the minds of decolonized peoples with Western technocratic culture, and, as this culture becomes more aggressive and more secular, it becomes less and less credible as a vehicle for the Good News of the Kingdom.

The Kingdom preached by Jesus Christ is mysterious and elusive. It catches people unaware (Matt 12:28). It is a spiritual movement which makes God truly King, because people submit to him in holiness and love. It allows God to reign over human hearts. As the preface (in the Roman Missal) for the feast of Christ the King puts it, it is an 'eternal and universal kingdom, a kingdom of truth and life, a kingdom of holiness and grace, a kingdom of justice, love and peace'. As such, it is a movement of unlimited scope and power. It challenges people and radically changes them. It promises them freedom of heart, strength of purpose and the prospect of a share in divine glory. Although its beginnings are unobtrusive, it is able to develop into an immense and powerful phenomenon, like yeast leavening dough or a mustard seed growing into a large shrub (Matt 13:31–33).

God's sovereignty over the world is to be established through his holy people, through the new Israel, the *qahal* or community founded by Jesus, whose leader is given the 'keys of the kingdom', to exercise authority, along with the other apostles, in the domain of faith (Matt 16:19–20; 18:18). The Church, therefore, is 'on earth the seed and the beginning of that kingdom'.[10] While Kingdom and Church are not to be equated, they are nevertheless inseparable. The Church is not an end in itself, but exists for the sake of the Kingdom, and is its indispensable instrument. Evangelization, therefore, is not identical with Church implantation, still less with a merely quantitative Church growth, but the community that is Church is necessarily and intimately oriented to the Kingdom. Evangelization, moreover, is essentially concerned with community-building, with changing hearts and improving lives. Evangelization is an invitation by the Church to stand with it and to work for the coming of the Kingdom.

The relationship between Church and Kingdom is a dynamic one. That is to say that the Church is on pilgrimage and grows and develops in accordance with the demands of the Kingdom.

The Kingdom is being established all over the world, in every country, nation, race, culture and language. It addresses every human context: sex, social class, political condition. The Church cannot afford to be static, but must adapt its institutions and structures to all these different and developing contexts. This does not mean that the Gospel is subject to change: Christ is the same yesterday, today and tomorrow. But it does mean that the Church's ministry, teaching and worship should be allowed to take on different forms and functions. The form taken by authority in the Church must never be allowed to become static, but should always be open to constructive, internal criticism. There is a necessary tension between what the Church is at any moment, and what it is called to become in obedience to its God-given vocation to serve the Kingdom.

We have seen that the 'little ones' have a privileged place in the Kingdom. Jesus himself chose the option for the poor and promised them a privileged place in the Kingdom. As the Beatitudes testify, the Kingdom belongs in a special way to the poor in spirit, to the gentle, to the merciful, to the peacemakers, to the seekers of justice, to the pure of heart, to the bereaved, to those who suffer violence. In his public life, we see Jesus constantly taking the side of the poor and disadvantaged, the sick and victims of discrimination, such as the tax collectors employed by the colonial administration, or those who were not sufficiently privileged to avoid incurring ritual impurity. Jesus' preference for the poor was part of the *kenosis* or self-emptying of the incarnate Son of God.

Later in this chapter we shall consider Gospel praxis or what is called 'the social Gospel', as an indispensable aspect of evangelization. Such an aspect is essentially bound up with the preferential option for the poor. This implies that the poor have a privileged role in the interpretation of the Gospel. They are evangelizers by definition, and the whole Church is evangelized by them. No one can evangelize others who is not first evangelized. The Gospel must be accepted, understood, lived before it can be transmitted to others, and this means listening in the first instance to the voice of the poor. God uses the poor and speaks through them to the Christian conscience. God loves the poor, and that is why the non-poor are committed to them, why they enter their world and espouse their cause. The poor speak to us of God's love for humanity, but they also speak to us of our inhumanity, and they set a concrete agenda for human love that aspires to become divine.

The preferential option which characterizes the Kingdom is an option for the whole Christian community. It does not in any way detract from the universal love to which all Christians are called. Jesus loved the rich young man and was at home in the house of

10

the rich Pharisee, yet he challenged them very sharply, in one case to become materially poor like himself, and in the other case to give the poor (represented by Jesus himself) respect (Mark 10:17–23; Luke 7:36–50). He was extremely scathing about those who placed their personal security in material possessions and neglected their neighbours who were poor. The poor, however, must also make this preferential option, as Gustavo Gutiérrez has pointed out.[11] While they do not deserve to be oppressed or to live in inhuman conditions, their ultimate salvation does not consist in becoming materially rich themselves.

Finally, God's Kingdom is necessarily centred on the person of a King. Jesus did not normally accept this title. He made his escape when the crowds wanted to make him king, because their idea of kingship was basically this-worldly. It was only when he stood broken and bleeding before Pilate, wearing the crown of thorns, that he accepted to be called king, but he immediately explained the title in a spiritual sense. Moreover, the same title was placed unequivocally on the very cross to which Jesus was nailed. In his earthly life Jesus was equally reluctant to use the royal title Messiah or Christ for the same reason, though he admitted the truth of Peter's confession (Matt 16:16–17; Mark 8:29). He drew attention to his miracles as signs of messianic fulfilment (Matt 11:4–8; Luke 7:22–23) and alluded to the messianic feast of heaven when he instituted the Eucharist (Mark 14:25).

Jesus identified with the coming Kingdom that he preached. It was the rule of God, transfiguring the present and orienting it towards an absolute future. To enter the Kingdom one had to listen to the voice of Jesus, to become his disciple. In fact, entry into the Kingdom was not a search on the part of humanity, but a call from God through Jesus. It is Jesus who makes the Kingdom present. He inaugurates it by revealing God as Father through word and action, by unfolding the demands of the Kingdom and by bringing liberation and salvation to the world. Through his death and resurrection Jesus fulfils the Kingdom, and shares universal power and authority with God over the world. God's reign is his reign, and he is proclaimed simply and definitely 'Lord'. There is a development of meaning from the earthly title 'Lord'/ 'Master' to the post-resurrection 'Lord', the title which had been used of Yahweh in the Old Testament and is now applied to Jesus.

The proclamation of the Good News of God's Kingdom is necessarily, therefore, the confession that Jesus is Lord and Universal King. The two things are inseparable. Proclaiming the reign of God means also proclaiming the reign of Jesus, whom God has made the Universal Lord and Christ. However, the Kingdom is not yet definitely established. It is still 'to come', and its final phase will coincide with the second coming of Jesus Christ in glory at the end of time. Until then, as history unfolds, the Kingdom is among us, beckoning us, surprising us, guiding us. As Church, we are pilgrims on the way to a growing maturity in Christ, as we strive towards greater conformity with the Kingdom of which we are called to be the sign and the seed.

Evangelization as proclamation

As we have already seen, proclamation is an aspect, albeit an indispensable one, of evangelization viewed as a form of communion or experiential sharing of the Good News of God's Kingdom, inaugurated by Jesus Christ. We have also seen that proclamation is not only verbal. However, the verbal dimension remains important and is invariably a component in other forms of communication and celebration. Verbal proclamation by definition relies on language; hence the importance of choosing the right language. Evangelizers cannot expect to be successful if they do not speak the language of the people they are sent to evangelize; and founders of missionary societies have often made this point.

One such founder was Cardinal Charles Lavigerie, who set up the Missionaries of Africa and the Missionary Sisters of Our Lady of Africa (better known as the White Fathers and White Sisters) in 1868 and 1869 respectively. Lavigerie directed that his missionaries – 'under pain of mortal sin' – should speak only the local language after six months, and that they should never use interpreters. He even demanded that his European missionaries speak only the local language among themselves, and not a Western language.[12] He laid down that his missionaries should undertake serious language study for two hours every day, writing grammars and dictionaries of hitherto unrecorded languages.[13] After this, they were to create small catechisms in the local language, and eventually translate the Gospels.[14]

As we shall see later, when we discuss inculturation, language is the principal cultural mechanism for the communication of meaning, so it was natural for Cardinal Lavigerie to urge his missionaries to go further than mere language learning and translation. He urged them to record the oral literature of the people they evangelized, their historical narratives, their myths and legends.[15] As a result, and in stark contrast to the popular image of the missionary as a cultural iconoclast, Lavigerie's followers laid the foundations of linguistic studies in Africa and collected a mass of ethnographic and literary material, especially proverbs, folktales and myths.

12

If language is important for the foreign missionary, it is equally important for the evangelizer at home. There are many pitfalls in using one's own mother tongue. A living language can quickly render Church formularies out of date. Languages are on the move, and evangelization must use the vocabulary and idiom of those it addresses. This is not only true for preaching, teaching and instructing, but also for Bible translation and liturgical language. Often there is a deep gulf between the literary culture of a preacher or teacher on the one hand, and that of the ordinary hearer on the other. Again, this is a question which shades into that of inculturation.

Verbal proclamation is mainly centred on the Sunday Scripture readings and homily, instructions on the occasion of celebrating the sacraments, religious education, Sunday School or catechism class. However, there are other forms in a literate and relatively affluent community, notably print media and broadcasting. The publishing of printed material is an important form of verbal proclamation. This includes book production, the Christian press and advertising. The subject of broadcasting and electronic media will be dealt with in Chapter 4 of this book. The main point at issue is whether filling the 'God-slot' on a commercial radio or TV system, or else choosing the expensive alternative of setting up one's own broadcasting system in competition, is likely to be an effective form of evangelization. Much depends on being in control of the medium one is using, of setting aside rivalry and directing the message to a receptive audience. This generally means being satisfied with a smaller-scale operation.

However, the Sunday homily has to compete with the expertise of professional communicators whom Christians are seeing every day in the media. Consequently, a premium must be placed on public speaking and preaching for those destined for the pastoral ministry. The liturgical homily must be short, centred on a single point and, as far as possible, narrative in form. It must be close to God's Word in the Sunday readings, close to the people's experience and express the preacher's own conviction. Finally, it must dispose the hearers for a fruitful sacramental celebration. All of this is uniquely difficult. The strength of the Catholic homiletic tradition lies in the fact that it eschews all histrionics which draw attention to the preacher and all forms of manipulation. It aims at a humble communication of the awesome truth.

Religious education and instructions for the sacraments need to obey ordinary pedagogical criteria in the first place. That is to say, they should be pupil-centred or life-centred, as well as God-centred, taking the life situation of the hearer as the starting-point and illuminating it by God's revelation. The hearer is thereby led to take a further step in his or her spiritual and sacramental life, and in membership of the Christian community. The aim is to help the hearer make a faith response under the impulse of the Spirit, and to construct his or her particular synthesis for living according to the dictates of the Kingdom.

Verbal proclamation can take the form of informal conversation. This happens when Christians give explicit witness to their faith on appropriate occasions in daily life. Generally, they are reticent about religious matters and are reluctant to speak openly about their religious beliefs and experiences. However, they need to be encouraged precisely to do this. A person who is deeply convinced of the truth and relevance of the Christian faith should not be embarrassed to speak about it, and even to suffer incomprehension and ridicule as a result, as long as there are also positive consequences. Nevertheless, there are occasions when no good can come of such witness, or when the negative results outweigh the positive. A necessary discernment has to be made. Individuals also now contribute to the Rite of Christian Initiation of Adults by informal verbal proclamation. They do this by accompanying the candidates, by serious exercise of their sponsorship, and by giving verbal encouragement and support.

Proclamation can be explicit without being verbal. This is especially the case with the visual arts. There is a parish in Kenya where Christians who are illiterate use a Bible picture series instead of the Bible itself, as an aid to contemplative prayer. Christian iconography is almost as old as the Gospels, and the statues, carvings, murals and stained glass of the medieval cathedrals and churches of Europe were known as 'the poor man's Bible'. Modern church buildings tend to be more sober in their decoration, but there is a growing need for pictorial communication in an age when people are losing the habit of reading, if they are not already semi-literate. This is the reason for the cartoon-strip Bibles, prayerbooks and saints' lives which are increasingly published.

Medieval Europe also produced a Christian theatre in which miracle plays and mystery plays nourished the faith and imagination of ordinary Christians. Dramatized Bible stories still play an important role in the proclamation of the Good News, particularly in countries of the non-Western world, and in the lives of the basic ecclesial communities. They are a powerful vehicle for dialogue between the lives of Christians and the Word of God. An important activity of the basic communities is the application of the Gospel message to daily life, and drama is a forceful aid to both the understanding of the text and its relevance to contemporary life. The use of electronic media in this context, provided there is scope for active participation and response, is a development of – but not really an adequate substitute for – the drama principle.

Poetry and song are further dimensions of verbal proclamation, although they can be said to overlap the worship aspect of evangelization. In most cultures music plays a vital role in speaking to the emotions and sensibilities of people, disposing them for prayer, for shared religious experiences and for the enhancement of meaning of sacred texts. Hymns and Gospel songs are a highly effective means of evangelization. In fact, the great hymn writer Charles Wesley produced a hymnal which was intended to be a complete compendium of Christian doctrine. Many ordinary Christians derive much of their understanding of Christianity from the texts of hymns, which shows that careful attention must be paid to their doctrinal content.

To music must be added dance. Sacred dance is far from out of place in the work of proclamation. Both in Europe and North America, where interpretative dance is largely a spectacle, rather than a fully participatory event, dance is coming to be accepted in religious contexts. In African cultures, dance is the height of cultural expression, and it is typically a community event, inviting maximum participation. As such, it possesses an ability to affect people very powerfully. In fact, it is rapidly becoming a liturgical and catechetical commonplace.

Having explored some of the various forms – verbal and non-verbal – which proclamation can take, we now turn to evangelization as praxis or witness.

Evangelization as praxis

We have already noted the intimate relationship between proclamation and praxis, and the constant emphasis of Jesus on the latter. Jesus condemned the hypocrite, the one who paid mere lip-service to the Word or who was not a 'doer of the Word'. It is clear from countless references in the New Testament that, according to Jesus, effective proclamation of the Gospel depends on putting the Gospel into practice. Of course, Jesus did acknowledge that theory and practice could become divorced, and that the behaviour of some religious leaders might be out of tune with their teaching. This was especially the case with the religious leaders of his own day. 'The scribes and the Pharisees are seated in the chair of Moses. You must obey them and follow everything they teach you to do; but do not imitate their actions, because they do not practise what they preach' (Matt 23:2–3).

However, Jesus also acknowledged that certain people who were not yet his disciples had faith or were capable of good works, without a clear understanding of his identity or message: people like the Roman centurion, the Syrophoenician woman, the rich young man. Such people possessed 'great faith' or were 'not far from the Kingdom'. They were seekers, whose good actions acquired meaning from the fullness of the truth, which he himself revealed. The man born blind witnessed that the one who had healed him came from God. To Jesus's question: 'Do you believe in the Son of Man?' he replied: 'Who is he, Lord, that I may believe in him?' (John 9:36). The father of the epileptic boy cried: 'I do believe, help thou my unbelief!' (Mark 9:24). This is not so very different from the exemplary agnostic who confides to a Christian that he envies his or her faith. Proclamation gives meaning to praxis, but praxis proves the validity of proclamation.

The point is that the message of Good News which is proclaimed cannot remain a mere theory. To become convincing, it must move from the theoretical to the practical level. The Word must be productive. It must produce visible and tangible fruit, and it is by the fruit that we shall know the nature of the producer (Matt 7:15–20). The chief fruit of evangelization is, of course, to verify that the Good News is really good, that it really does bring life and hope to people, that it really does bring them peace and justice, that it really does gather people in the forgiveness of God. The news we bring points to the triumph of good and the overthrow of evil; and it invites the believer to join this struggle which helps fulfil the Kingdom. The proclamation of the Good News, therefore, inaugurates a process of liberation and bestows the gift of life and of salvation, and this is the outcome of faith in Jesus.

The Good News is addressed, in the first place, to the poor. 'The poor have the Gospel preached to them,' Jesus told the emissaries of John the Baptist (Luke 7:22). In the synagogue at Nazareth Jesus read Isaiah's prophecy: 'He has chosen me to bring good news to the poor', and told his hearers that it was now fulfilled (Luke 4:18). The poor are defined descriptively by Jesus in the Beatitudes and in his tableau of the last judgement. They are the materially and spiritually poor. They include those who mourn, those who are meek, those who hunger and thirst for justice, those who show mercy to others, those who preserve purity of heart and those who try to make peace. Above all, they involve those who are insulted and persecuted because they are followers of Jesus (Matt 5:1–11). The poor also comprise the stranger – the migrant and the refugee – those threatened with hunger and food shortage, the naked and needy, the sick and dying, those imprisoned justly or unjustly (Matt 25:31–46).

We can discover the nature of the poor from the people with whom Jesus associated in his earthly life. They were generally people suffering from social stigma, despised foreigners like the Samaritans, the Syrophoenicians whom the Jews called 'dogs', the unwelcome Romans; the ritually impure, the colonial collaborators – the tax collectors. Worst of all the social outcasts were the lepers and those suffering from virulent diseases of the skin. There were also epileptics, the deaf and dumb, the blind, the paralysed and the disabled. Jesus spent the greater part of his public life in the company of such people. Even the twelve special companions he chose reflected this predilection. They came, like himself, from 'Galilee of the gentiles', that area of Jewish and pagan syncretism. They were labourers and fisherfolk, and they even included Matthew, a tax collector, and Simon, a Zealot or guerrilla fighter, whose duty it presumably was to kill people like Matthew.

At St Anne's in the old city of Jerusalem can be seen the excavations of the probatic pool, where Jesus cured the paralysed man (John 5:1–18). It was 'a pool with five porches', with 'sick people lying in the porches', waiting for the movement of water. The ruins of the temple reservoirs, called the pool of the Sheep Gate or Bethzatha, bear no trace of porches or porticoes. However, alongside the double pool is a series of semi-subterranean chambers through which water was piped. In these chambers archaeologists have found *ex voto* objects and other evidence of a cult of Aesculapius, the Roman god of healing. It looks as if these were the porches of John's Gospel and that the 'angel' who stirred the water was a pagan god. If so, it demonstrates the kind of syncretism and popular superstition indulged in by those whom Jesus frequented. Jesus was apparently no purist, no stickler for niceties of form. The poor he chose were those whom the establishment despised.

In the next chapter, we shall look at evangelization from the point of view of liberation. Jesus's option for the poor was directed towards their liberation, and this is the overall purpose of the Gospel. 'If you obey my word, you will be my disciples; you will know the truth and the truth will set you free' (John 8:31–32). Jesus came to liberate the poor, to give the blind sight, to set free the captive and the oppressed. He relieved human suffering, because it was a symptom and a symbol of a deeper sickness – the sickness of the human spirit. That is why he was not content merely to heal physically, but himself drew near to the world of suffering. His Kingdom spells liberation from every kind of evil and offers hope to every category of suffering and deprived humanity. The Gospel is the Good News of a new possibility from God, enabling us to share in his wholeness and holiness.

True evangelization does not isolate people or cause them to withdraw from active life in their community. It does not create a ghetto in which people are insulated against the perverse influences of the outside world. On the contrary, it involves people, and reinserts them in their world as agents of beneficial change. An evangelization which ignores the social character of the Gospel plays into the hands of the oppressor, and disenfranchises the poor. True evangelization, on the other hand, empowers the poor and emphasizes their birthright as human beings to share in the good things which this world provides.

The Gospel is not simply a question of words or of doctrinal propositions. It is essentially a way of life – a praxis – which is there to be lived by people. In God himself word and act are indistinguishable. His word, or *memra*, to use the Hebrew term, is creative. It brings into existence whatever it names. It effects whatever it expresses. The Gospel is God's word, the Good News about the incarnated Word. It is also a plan of action, a challenge to commitment, *metanoia* or conversion of life. It reveals the risen Christ acting through the Spirit in our midst, and invites our co-operation and discipleship.

Evangelization as praxis is community-building. Its first consequence is to bring into existence a community of faith and of salvation. This community is itself evangelized, and becomes, in its turn, evangelizing. That is why, whenever we speak of evangelization, we are also speaking of community-building. A person becomes a Christian and submits to the Gospel by entering a community of faith. A Christian becomes an evangelizer and proclaims the Good News of the Kingdom, in so far as he or she belongs to this community of faith. According to the Gospel outlook, the Christian treats all fellow human beings as 'neighbours', persons to be respected, not tools to be used, or objects to be exploited. Evangelization is not an individualistic activity, carried out on the initiative and responsibility of a single person. It is conducted in the name of a community and is somehow always linked to this community. It arises in community and goes on to create community.

The Christian community is built on foundations of mutual trust, self-revelation and active love. In fact, love is the community virtue above all others. It could be said that evangelization is no more nor less than loving, and this is the way Mother Teresa of Calcutta, for example, likes to define missionary evangelization. Mission is an eminent way of fulfilling Christ's 'great' or 'new' commandment – to love other human beings with the selfsame love with which God loves us.

An over-emphasis on verbal proclamation exposes the evangelizer to charges of proselytism when humanitarian works of mercy or development aid are also carried out. An interest in helping the victims of oppression or the casualties of war and natural disasters can be represented as – and may indeed become – a form of bribery, promising material advantages to those who embrace the Gospel. Such bribery may even be justified in certain fundamentalist circles on the grounds that material prosperity is a reward of faith. Apart from bringing evangelization into disrepute, such a procedure produces the proverbial 'rice Christians', those who are faithful only as long as they enjoy the material benefits provided by the evangelizer. It is clear that, just as the Good News is addressed to everyone, whether or not there is a response, so the active love of the evangelizer is directed towards everyone, whether or not they become Christian. God's love is universal.

The proclamation of God's love, therefore, demands the practice of that love, if it is to be at all effective. God loves humanity through evangelization. Not only is his love revealed, but it is also felt. Probably the most common reason for rejecting the Gospel when it is preached is the observed discrepancy between the content of the message and the example given by the messenger. We know that bad example does not invalidate the truth of the message, but it renders evangelization incomplete, and is an obstacle to its success.

Evangelization as prayer

It is important to distinguish between 'prayer' and 'prayers'. Prayer (singular) is the living communion of the believer with God, perceived as present in the social relationships and experiences of humanity. Prayers (plural) are the techniques of communication, mental, oral, written, which the believer employs to express this communion of life. A prayer literature offers evidence about the nature of prayer, but the latter is primary. What is important is 'the raising of the heart and mind to God' – prayer as life, prayer as ongoing experience. This state of communion is achieved through explicit union with God in moments of formal communication (prayers), in sacramental action, in explicit acts of discernment in everyday life, but it is basically a person's underlying disposition. Praying is no more nor less than loving God. Prayer is therefore not merely an aspect of evangelization, but its fundamental condition or mode. Extending the Kingdom of God cannot take place without the basic disposition that we call prayer.

Different authors assign particular meanings to words such as 'prayer' or 'worship'. We have given a threefold definition of evangelization as: proclamation, praxis and prayer. Another formula might be: word, witness and worship, and some might prefer the word 'worship' for the fundamental doxological attitude of the believer towards God. Such a usage is perfectly legitimate, but the word 'worship' is probably more often used to refer to the liturgical complex of ritual actions, verbal formulas, readings and instructions which give expression to religious adoration. The disposition or attitude, which we prefer to call 'prayer', is at the heart of such a complex, and validates it.

As we have seen, in dealing with evangelization as proclamation, the liturgy is an obvious context for evangelization. The Word is proclaimed and celebrated in worship. Religious beliefs are affirmed and communicated. The liturgy possesses a very real catechetical and missionary function, as the history of many conversions testifies. This is exactly as it should be. The power of example is especially attractive in the area of worship, because it communicates sincerity and conviction. Christian evangelizers have always been respected among peoples of other faiths, when their acts of worship have been visible.

Some evangelizers have even suggested that catechesis be removed altogether from the classroom, and that it is impossible to evoke a faith-response from the student through explanatory and discursive lessons. Instead they have advocated a catechesis through prayer, which would give the student real conviction and a true religious sense. At any rate, the initiation to prayer should be an important part of any catechesis. Schooling people in prayer is an essential aspect of evangelization itself, if its purpose is to help people encounter God and enter his Kingdom. Christians in general know very little about prayer and about techniques of prayer. They need to deepen their life of prayer and their experience of God, if they are to be fully evangelized, and become, in their turn, evangelizers.

Nevertheless, the evangelistic value of prayer and worship is not merely a question of giving example. Nor is it merely a successful catechetical technique. Much more than this, worship is the realm of encounter with the divine mystery, the psycho-social zone in which God is the dominant partner. Once mind and heart are raised to him, new insights are revealed and new levels of conviction and commitment are attained. Worship is prophetical because it enables the believer to transcend ordinary needs and concerns. It is truly evangelizing because it sets the scene for the human encounter with God.

Just as prayer is the heart of worship, it is also the starting-point for all evangelization. This is because the process of evangelization is not owned or directed by Christians, but by God. The

Kingdom belongs to God and is extended in accordance with his will. What the evangelizer says or does, therefore, will only be valid and effective if it is said or done in accordance with God's will. The fundamental motivation of the evangelizer is to be in living communion with the object of faith, that is, possessing the disposition of prayer. It is prayer which puts the evangelizer in touch with the real movement of growth in the Kingdom, and with the divine source of energy and initiative.

In Chapter 3 we shall consider the triple vocation of the Christian, in local and global mission, and in the vocation of contemplation. It may seem surprising to refer to the vocation of contemplation as a form of evangelization. Yet, in the light of the foregoing discussion, it is entirely justified. The main work of the contemplative is the *opus Dei*, or 'God's work', the task of giving expression to the prayerful communion with God which is the spiritual life of the Christian. The contemplative enters into the very heart and reality of evangelization, building God's Kingdom through prayer.

There are numerous examples of contemplatives who saw their vocation in this light. They were people who understood the power of prayer to build the Kingdom of God, and whose lives were lived at the heart of the Church's mission. The most outstanding example is that of Saint Thérèse of Lisieux, the contemplative nun whom Pius XI declared to be Patroness of the Missions. It is the teaching of the Second Vatican Council, in the decree on the renewal of religious life, *Perfectae Caritatis*, that the more fervently religious join themselves to Christ by the gift of their whole life, the fuller does the Church's life become and the more fruitful its apostolate.[16] Thus contemplation not only strengthens evangelization and sustains the efforts of evangelizers, but it really participates in Christ's redemptive work itself.

The Christian life is a life of prayer. It is a communion with God, in which the believer praises the Creator and expresses dependence on him. This is done through Christ, in the power of the Spirit. It is living under the reign of God, being a part of his Kingdom. Extending God's Kingdom is part and parcel of the Christian life, and is carried forward with and through prayer. Evangelization is unthinkable without prayer, and inseparable from prayer.

The new evangelization

In his encyclical letter *Redemptoris Missio*, Pope John Paul II uttered the evocative phrase 'new or second evangelization'.[17] It is a phrase which has struck a chord throughout the Catholic Church, and which has given rise to several dynamic interpretations. We shall return to the concept again in Chapter 3, but it is worthwhile examining it in this introductory chapter, since its appeal relates to the concept of evangelization itself. In fact, it can be truthfully said that genuine evangelization is always profoundly new.

The expression was first coined by Pope John Paul II in an address given at Port-au-Prince, Haiti, in 1983. The Pope spoke of a 'commitment... not of re-evangelization, but of a new evangelization – new in its fervour, in its methods and in its expression'.[18] Seven years later, in *Redemptoris Missio*, he spoke of the need for a 'new or second evangelization' in countries where whole groups of the faithful have lost a living sense of the faith, or even no longer consider themselves Christians.

The Pope was clearly envisaging the problem of post-Christian secularism in the technological cultures of the Western industrialized world; but he was also considering countries in which Christianity had not taken firm root from the beginning, places in which the faith had not made significant headway. It is striking that the Pope rejects the term 're-evangelization' and opts for the phrase 'new or second evangelization'. In other words, he is speaking about a real evangelization, not some kind of additional update. This new or second evangelization is needed either because the original evangelization has lost its momentum, or because it was in some sense flawed.

This is the case, Leonardo Boff argues, with the original evangelization of Latin America.[19] This was not a truly liberative evangelization, but one which sought to transplant the institutions, images, concepts and moral habits of European Christian culture to the Americas. There was no genuine encounter between the Gospel and the religious cultures of the native American peoples. The official Church of Latin America remained European in outlook and expression, but there was a marginal, popular form of Christianity which was more creative and authentic. What is now needed is a new start, a fresh departure from within the religious cultures of the Latin American poor.

This critique is really saying that the first evangelization was not sufficiently new or original, or that it has failed to take account of new situations and changed circumstances. The second evangelization needs to be entirely new. It must be accompanied by a new fervour. It must be an evangelization which is new in its methods and its expression. In fact, its newness is a mark of its genuineness.

No movement or period of evangelization is perfect; nor is it ever fully achieved in a permanent and unalterable fashion. The Gospel of Christ cannot be domesticated. On the contrary, it continues to challenge the Christian community. Moreover, this community itself is subject to profound social and structural changes. Human groupings can change their identity, can coalesce with one another, or even disappear altogether. They are not static and unchanging. As soon as the boast is made that evangelization is complete, history gives it the lie. How many times in Christian history has the Church been overtaken by events, or been slow to adapt to the changed realities of human living? Even more to the point, to claim that the work of evangelization is complete is to misunderstand the nature of the Gospel and the Kingdom, which themselves are developing and unfolding realities.

No doubt, continuity is also important, but evangelization needs to be constantly renewed, if it is to be creative and relevant. In some cases – perhaps in Latin America, as well as in North America – there is a more urgent need for a new or second evangelization, but in every situation the newness of the Gospel should be communicated and felt, bringing about a new fervour. It is this fervour which enables Christians to confront obstacles, solve problems and overcome dangers in the spreading of God's Kingdom.

In catechetical circles it is customary to speak about 'pre-evangelization' and 'primary evangelization'. Pre-evangelization refers to the process of preparing the ground for the explicit proclamation of the Gospel, but it is already by implication a real evangelization.[20] Some years ago, a Catholic missionary society was beginning work among the nomads of northern Kenya. It was proposed to spend three to four years making contact with the people, studying them and researching their social and cultural life before beginning evangelization proper. This was an excellent suggestion, but it was pointed out to them that their very presence among the nomads was already the start of the evangelization process, which could not, in fact, be postponed once it had begun.

Primary evangelization refers to the early stages of evangelization, when the Christian community is still very small and the Church is as yet undeveloped. It is a period that demands specialized missionary skill, as we shall see more particularly in Chapter 2. This phase of evangelization has been called by Pope John Paul II the *missio ad gentes*, or 'mission to the nations'.[21] Missionaries have a preference for 'primary tasks', although – as we shall see – this does not exhaust the concerns of a missionary vocation. Within any human context there is a scale of priorities, and primary evangelization is a missionary priority.

It is clear that, following Pope John Paul's reference to situations in which people no longer consider themselves to be Christian, it can be argued that there is little or no difference in practice between primary evangelization on the one hand, and new or second evangelization on the other. At any rate, primary evangelization has the potential to be radically new, and this is what is needed in the situations addressed by the new evangelization. This leads us on to a discussion about the dialogue between the Gospel and cultural realities, which was the point of departure for this chapter and which is the subject of the following one.

References

1 One thinks, for example, of the writings of Don Cupitt.
2 J. Hick and P. Knitter (eds), *The Myth of Christian Uniqueness* (Maryknoll, NY: Orbis Books, 1987); G. D'Costa (ed.), *Christian Uniqueness Reconsidered* (Maryknoll, NY: Orbis Books, 1990).
3 Cf. *Redemptoris Missio*, 17. The encyclical does not name the proponents of this view, but Cardinal Jozef Tomko, in an unpublished report dated April 1991, 'The Challenge of the Sects and the News of the One and Only Saviour', does not hesitate to mention Michael Amaladoss SJ and J. Kavunka SVD as proponents of theocentric and Kingdom-centred theories.
4 Cf. V. Donovan, *Christianity Rediscovered* (London: SCM Press, 1978).
5 Cf. Leonardo Boff, *New Evangelization* (Maryknoll, NY: Orbis Books, 1991), p. 118.
6 E. Schillebeeckx, *Christ: The Christian Experience in the Modern World* (London: SCM Press, 1980), p. 30.
7 For a full discussion of the scope of these two terms and the relationship between them, cf. David Bosch, *Transforming Mission* (Maryknoll, NY: Orbis Books, 1991), pp. 409–20.
8 Cf. John Paul II, *Redemptoris Missio*, 44.
9 Cf. *The Tablet* (10 October 1991), p. 1282.
10 *Lumen Gentium*, 5.
11 G. Gutiérrez, 'Gustavo Gutiérrez Speaks to the M.I.L.', *The Missionary Institute Record*, no. 1 (1989), p. 16.
12 *Instructions aux Missionaires* (Namur, 1950), pp. 28, 134.
13 Ibid., p. 70.
14 Ibid., pp. 70–1.
15 Ibid., pp. 115–16.
16 *Perfectae Caritatis*, 1.
17 *Redemptoris Missio*, 33.

18 Quoted by Leonardo Boff, op. cit., p. xii.
19 Boff, ibid.
20 Bosch, op. cit., p. 412, objects to such terms as 'pre-evangelization', and sees them all as implied in 'evangelism'. Personally, I still find them useful.
21 Cf. *Redemptoris Missio, passim.*

2   Integral elements of evangelization

An evangelization experience

The ten years (1968–77) which I spent at the Pastoral Institute of
Eastern Africa, at Gaba, in Uganda, were important years for me
personally.[1] They were also important years for the whole Church.
I joined the Institute two years after the closing of the Second
Vatican Council, and our mandate was to help form key Christians
who could understand and carry forward the renewal of the Catholic Church in Africa. It was a time of optimism, imagination and
creativity. It was also a time when the methodology of religious
education was changing. Some of us – like myself – who joined
the Institute's staff at its opening in early 1968 knew little about
catechetics, or indeed about educational method in general. However, we had all heard of 'dialogue', the most celebrated Vatican II
catchword.

Much of what we tried to do at Gaba could be described as the
application of dialogue, a reciprocal communication leading
towards a common goal. Lay people, religious, priests – and even
sometimes bishops – engaged in dialogue there. Staff and students
held dialogue with one another. There was also dialogue with
African tradition; and the Vatican Secretariat for Non-Christians,
nowadays called the Pontifical Council for Interreligious Dialogue,
held a meeting at Gaba in 1974 with representatives of African
traditional religions. Later in the same year we became involved
in preparing the episcopal delegates from eastern Africa to the
1974 Synod of Bishops on Evangelization. This was, perhaps, one
of the most important Rome synods, which saw the African bishops opt for an 'incarnation' of the Church in their continent, and
which resulted in the Apostolic Exhortation on evangelization,
Evangelii Nuntiandi (1975). 'Incarnation' was soon to be known
by the more technical term 'inculturation'.

By the time that the 1974 Synod met, we at Gaba Pastoral

Institute had evolved our own ideas about religious education, particularly where adults were concerned. We were convinced that the Christian faith was 'caught not taught', and the syllabuses we created for African secondary schools took the students' own experience and aspirations as the starting point for exploring a variety of life-themes in the light of biblical theology and Church history. Our aim was to promote a dialogue between revelation and experience, which would result in the students evolving their own faith synthesis.

Dialogue was even more explicit in adult catechesis. Our aim was to set up a joint study, a common enterprise of catechist and catechumens and/or adult Christians, exploring the mutual relationship between the Christian message and the experience of the group. The need for working in groups became more and more clear to us, and we saw the adult group as normative for others at the lower age levels. Little by little, we realized that we could no longer merely lecture about such a methodology to our students at the Pastoral Institute. We had to use the method ourselves in our own teaching. This decision brought about a revolution in the Institute's syllabus, and in our own classroom technique. Teaching, or better, 'guided learning', became an experience of creative listening, of community-building, of mutual Christian formation.

Some of us travelled to catechetical meetings in Latin America and South East Asia. There we learned that the emphasis on group work and community-building was a function of liberation theology, and that community members could be empowered by the Gospel to free themselves from sources of oppression within and outside themselves. The yearning for liberation had been experienced historically in the abolition of slavery, in decolonization and in the civil rights movement. The Gospel of Jesus Christ was increasingly being seen as the 'truth [that] sets you free' (John 8:31) – free from personal and social sin, free from the suffering and social oppression which is the consequence of sin.

Such ideas bore fruit at Gaba in the emphasis we began to place on building communities, an emphasis that found an echo in the pastoral planning of the bishops of eastern Africa, and in the priority they placed on building small Christian communities. This programme was intended to help African Christians live and practise their faith in their own life contexts, without making them rigidly conform to Church structures imposed on them from above. The primary – the basic – reality of Church was to be experienced at the small community level, rather than at the level of outstation or parish.

In our efforts to carry out the teaching of the Second Vatican

Council, and to apply it to the concrete and complex situations of the Church in eastern Africa, we found ourselves developing a theology of evangelization, a theory of how to spread the Good News of God's Kingdom. We discovered that there are three integral elements in evangelization: dialogue, inculturation and liberation. These three elements constantly overlap and illuminate each other.

When we speak of dialogue nowadays, we usually refer to interfaith or interreligious dialogue, and also to ecumenical dialogue. As we shall see, this is an important aspect of evangelization. However, the word 'dialogue' also refers to inculturation, which is nothing more nor less than the ongoing dialogue of faith and culture. Liberation can also be seen as the outcome of a dialogue between the Gospel and the concrete circumstances of people's lives. Religious systems are essentially cultural systems, and many traditional cultures are also correctly described as 'religious cultures'. This explains why inter-faith dialogue and inculturation normally overlap. Furthermore, these elements imply the liberation of faith and culture. Finally, in certain instances, where Christians are persecuted or oppressed by non-Christian religious regimes, inter-faith dialogue may have a special relevance for liberation.

In this chapter we shall explore the nature, relevance and interrelationships of these three integral elements of evangelization: inculturation, dialogue and liberation. The anthropological definition of culture is all-embracing. It includes religion as well as the social, political and economic contexts of human life. Inculturation is therefore basic to the other two elements, and will be treated first in the following discussion.

The Church and cultures

Inculturation is an integral element of evangelization. Gerald Arbuckle goes so far as to say: inculturation 'is synonymous with evangelization'.[2] In other words, a merely external or superficial evangelization is no evangelization at all. Individuals must be evangelized within their cultures and not be treated as having no culture at all, which simply means that they become the victims of aggression by an alien culture. Twelve years ago, the Zaïrean theologian Oscar Bimwenyi lamented that African Christians are obliged to pray to God with a liturgy that is not theirs, to live a morality which takes no account of their own life context, to follow a Canon Law which has nothing to do with African juridical realities, and to reflect on the truths of faith using the philosophical and theological categories of the other Christian communities which evangelized them.[3]

Leonardo Boff tells the same story when he recounts the history of the 'colonial evangelization' of Latin America.[4] This evangelization included a great deal of violence. There was no dialogue, no mutual listening, no reciprocal learning. There was just direct domination by the European invaders, undoing by bad example what the missionaries taught by their catechesis. Indigenous culture was deliberately undermined. The people were enslaved; their material possessions seized. On the one hand, they were required to accept the Christian Gospel; on the other, the rule of the Iberian monarchs. The African captives who were brought by the heinous slave traffickers to the New World were also forcibly robbed of their culture, and could only preserve their traditional beliefs by giving them an outward appearance of Catholicism in the syncretic cults which survive to this day in places like Brazil and Haiti. Such are the sad consequences of an evangelization which does not dialogue with the culture of those it addresses.

Culture is part of the human phenomenon. Its discovery as an empirical reality is one of the achievements of the twentieth century. This derives from the awareness that everything a human being thinks or does is an aspect of a pattern or whole.[5] The perception of a variety of patterns in human thought and behaviour occurs wherever people come into contact with a set of alien or foreign conventions. The rise of modern nationalisms, followed by the revolution in transport and communication, has forced us to take such differences seriously. Because we can only experience other cultures as an extension of our own, we are forced to invent our understanding of them, but we do so in a relatively objective manner, along the lines of observing and learning, and not as a kind of free fantasy.[6] We tend to see other cultures as mirrors or creative analogues of our own conceptual system. No doubt, this may be a handicap from the point of view of objectivity, but it imparts a degree of relativity to the cultures that we identify.[7]

The recognition of cultural pluralism may be a Western scientific necessity, but it is also the outcome of political self-determination and self-assertion in the face of colonial annexation, and of resistance to assimilation or domination by alien systems. In contemporary Africa, for example, 'culture' is an emotive term. Africans, like their black cousins in the Americas, are concerned to recover or redefine their traditional culture. Asian countries also are often characterized by a defiant, and frequently anti-Western, religious culture. Today we are also witnessing the dissolution of the Eastern European bloc into an assemblage of national and even ethnic identities.

Culture is a comprehensive concept which embraces all that individuals acquire or learn as members of a human society. One of the functions of culture is to help people relate cognitively, affectively and behaviourally to experience. Culture offers a pattern of meanings embodied in images or symbols. These control the individual's perception of reality. Culture also results in the creation of a group identity and of an adaptive strategy for living and surviving.

In general, Catholic writers prefer the term 'culture', but there are those who favour 'context', and who like to speak about 'contextualization', rather than about inculturation. This is partly because they would restrict the term 'culture' to such things as folklore or the arts and because they wish to place an emphasis on modernity, technology and socio-political realities. It is also acknowledged that 'inculturation' was a sociological term before it became a commonplace of Catholic theology. There is, however, a difficulty about defining the term 'context'. Contexts are complex, diverse and indeterminate. Moreover, anthropologists would argue that the theory of culture is sufficiently comprehensive to embrace modernity and the political scene. For these reasons, culture seems to be a more workable concept.[8]

The Church's understanding of culture has evolved, together with that of humanity at large. Originally, culture was conceived as a single, universal, normative criterion, according to which human beings were adjudged 'cultured' or 'uncultured'. This is what Bernard Lonergan called the 'classicist assumption'.[9] Christianity in its Latin form was deemed to be the perfection of this culture of humanity, and the Church was thus identified with the world as such. Evangelization was characterized by a Eurocentric mono-culturalism.

At the theoretical level, though not yet at the practical, mono-culturalism has now been displaced by the empirical, pluralistic understanding of culture, which has been described above. First Pius XII, and then with greater clarity John XXIII, referred in official documents to a plurality of cultures.[10] This prepared the way for an important theme of the Second Vatican Council, which was that the recipients of the Gospel

> constitute large and distinct groups united by enduring cultural ties, ancient religious traditions, and strong social relationships.[11]

This concept of the large cultural grouping developed into the 'socio-cultural region', associated, if not identified, by the Council's missionary decree, with the particular Church.[12] Finally, the

Vatican Council turned its attention to culture as such, in the Pastoral Constitution on the Church in the Modern World.

> ... culture necessarily has historical and social overtones,
> and the word 'culture' often carries with it sociological
> and ethnological connotations; in this sense one can speak
> about a plurality of cultures. For different styles of living
> and different scales of values originate in different ways of
> using things, of working and self-expression, of practising
> religion and of behaviour, of establishing laws and juridical
> institutions, of developing science and the arts and of
> cultivating beauty. Thus the heritage of its institutions forms
> the patrimony proper to each human community; thus,
> too, is created a well-defined, historical milieu which
> envelops the men of every nation and age, and from which
> they draw the values needed to foster humanity and
> civilization.[13]

The Council document then went on to consider the relationship between faith and culture, and more particularly between the Gospel and culture. The Christian who is active in the life of human social groups is contributing to the perfection of creation.[14] The universal mission of the Church entails communion among a plurality of cultures that is mutually enriching.

> ... the Church has been sent to all ages and nations and,
> therefore, is not tied exclusively and indissolubly to any
> race or nation, to any one particular way of life, or to
> any customary practices, ancient or modern. The Church
> is faithful to its traditions and is at the same time conscious
> of its universal mission; it can, then, enter into communion
> with different forms of culture, thereby enriching both itself
> and the cultures themselves.[15]

Such ideas bore fruit during the 1974 Synod of Bishops when demands were made for a more thoroughgoing cultural 'incarnation' of theology and evangelization, notably by the bishops of Africa and Madagascar. After an initial hesitation by Paul VI, this request was answered positively in the Apostolic Exhortation *Evangelii Nuntiandi*. In this document the Pope spoke of the need to transpose the Gospel into a language that is 'anthropological and cultural', rather than 'semantic or literary', and to evangelize cultures,

> not in a purely decorative way as it were by applying a
> thin veneer, but in a vital way, in depth and right to their
> very roots.[16]

It was inevitable that these ideas should converge at the 1977 Synod with developments in the field of catechesis. The catechetical congress at Eichstatt in 1960 formulated basic principles of missionary catechetics, and these received local application in the congresses of Bangkok 1962, Katigondo 1964, Manila 1966 and finally Medellín 1969. Through these meetings, the concept of an experiential or life-approach catechesis came to be widely accepted in the Church and to be sanctioned by the Rome catechetical congress of 1971. At the same time, the concept of 'inculturation', and even the term itself, were brought into currency by the Society of Jesus in the years following the 1974 Synod. Pedro Arrupe's 'Letter to the Whole Society on Inculturation' appeared in April 1978, eighteen months before John Paul II took up the term in *Catechesi Tradendae*.[17] Since then, inculturation has become a commonplace of contemporary theology, although the catechetical convergence of the 1970s has been replaced by the increasingly divergent emphases of official, or Roman, teaching on the one hand, and the perceptions of writers in non-Western local Churches on the other.

The meaning of inculturation

'Inculturation' is a term that denotes the presentation and re-expression of the Gospel in forms and terms proper to a culture, processes which result in the reinterpretation of both, without being unfaithful to either.[18] It is a creative development which, as the International Theological Commission rightly says, participates in the dynamism of cultures and their intercommunication.[19] Definitions of inculturation tend to put the emphasis on one or other term of the equation – Gospel or culture. Here are examples of both:

> The process of a deep, sympathetic adaptation to, and appropriation of, a local culture in which the Church finds itself, in a way that does not compromise its basic faith.[20]

> The process by which a particular people respond to the saving Word of God and express their response in their own cultural forms of worship, reflection, organization and life. This is how a local church is born and continues to live.[21]

Inculturation is a process which involves the destigmatization of alien cultures, and the self-emptying (*exinanitio sui ipsius*) of both the evangelizer and evangelized cultures.[22] Several writers make much of the fact that inculturation helps cultures to transcend their own limits. In fact, the ultimate criterion of inculturation is interculturation, or transculturation.[23] However, cultures are already by definition categories of interaction, and evangelization merely intensifies and canalizes their intercommunication.

Closely associated with inculturation is the problem variously described as 'culturalism', 'over-inculturation' or simply 'syncretism'.[24] Acculturation is necessarily accompanied by a greater or lesser degree of syncretism, or anomalous conflict of meaning. For Christian writers, syncretism occurs when a culture appropriates the Gospel and distorts its meaning, or when unabsorbed cultural elements with conflicting meanings are juxtaposed with Gospel values.[25] In so far as inculturation is concerned, syncretism must not be allowed to invalidate the Gospel. Inculturation, therefore, implies a measure of desyncretization, and this was the experience of the earliest Christians in their efforts to detach themselves from Judaic religious culture. Today we observe many Christian syncretisms: South African apartheid, new religious movements or sects, Western politicians claiming the 'moral high ground', or Christianity allied to political nationalisms. Eugene Uzukwu has discovered an 'operative theology of identity between the priestly and hierarchical model of the Church' and the worship of spirits and taking of titles among the Igbo of Nigeria.[26] Nearly twenty years ago Philip Turner discovered a similar Christian syncretism in the kingdoms of Uganda.[27] William Biernatski points out that syncretism occurs when enthusiastic missionaries conduct a superficial adaptation in ignorance of the true meaning of cultural symbols, and Lamin Sanneh shows that cultural domination has also been a cause of syncretism, particularly in Latin America.[28] Robert Schreiter takes a sympathetic view of syncretism and has been criticized for this.[29] But it is clear that syncretism is present to a greater or lesser degree in every form of Christianity from New Testament times.[30] Inculturation is a task always yet to be achieved, because it involves a never-ending appeal to cultural conversion.[31] In the nature of things, we are obliged to remain within what John Coleman calls 'the realm of *towards* discourse', where inculturation is concerned.[32] There is no ready-made model for Christian cultures, least of all the Euro-American model, so often presented as a model of successful inculturation.[33] As Lesslie Newbigin remarked, 'The Gospel escapes domestication!'[34]

Christological bases of inculturation

There are a number of possible starting-points or bases for a theology of inculturation. The late D. S. Amalorpavadass suggested four: creation and history, incarnation and the Paschal Mystery, the universal mission of the Church, authentic tradition and the ordinary *magisterium*.[35] Although he has not made the theology of the local Church one of his starting-points, the last two belong to the realm of ecclesiology and it is here that the problem of translating inculturation theory into evangelizing practice is at its most acute. Before tackling the ecclesiological problem, let us look briefly at the first two suggested points of departure.

The Second Vatican Council resurrected a dynamic phrase, coined by St Justin Martyr, that of the *semina verbi*, or 'seeds of the Word'. The phrase occurs in two passages of the missionary decree.[36] In the first instance, it is used in much the same way as Justin himself used it. In the second instance it has been somewhat devalued to stand for a dubious Gospel essence which acquires exterior form from the cultural soil in which it has been planted.[37] In Justin's original use of the image, the seed was not the explicit proclamation of the Gospel, but the mysterious influence of the eternal Logos, of whom it was said 'through him all things came to be' (John 1:3). Justin's concept of Logos or Divine Reason had its antecedents in the Stoic concept of a worldwide intelligent principle, in the hypostatized wisdom of biblical sapiential literature, in the personified creative *memra* of rabbinical writings and in the Johannine Logos which affirmed the previous divine existence of Jesus and his intimate association with the creative work of God.[38] According to the teaching of Justin, the Logos is 'seed-bearing' (*spermatikos*), and all human cultural traditions are granted a share in, or seed of, this Logos. This enables them to see reality darkly before it is enlightened for them by the proclamation of the incarnate Word. The Logos is God's agent in creation and it also exists throughout the world in disseminated form. Justin would have agreed with John Henry Newman that 'No people (to speak in general terms) has been denied a revelation from God'.[39]

St Justin's concept of the world-seeding Logos was used by St Clement of Alexandria and the other Apologist Fathers of the second century, in the first dialogue between Christianity in its existing Hellenistic-Jewish form and the pagan cultural traditions of the Mediterranean. It has reappeared in the creation theology of our own day, with its concern for the care of the Earth.[40] According to to this theology the 'within-ness' dimension of reality reflects the identification of God-in-Christ with his emergent creation, and redemption is the restoration of divine harmony in the world.[41] The theology of the environment thus joins forces with inculturation theology and with the theology of religions in its effort to trace the history of revelation in non-Christian religious traditions. An African theologian, Efoé-Julien Pénoukou of Benin, has drawn the logical conclusion that the proclamation of the Good News about Jesus Christ does not outmode these traditions, but gladly recognizes the truths they contain. The Christian conversion of culture is merely a further, yet definitive, step in the espousing of particular cultures by God.[42]

The analogy between the Incarnation of Jesus Christ and 'the more profound adaptation' which today we call 'inculturation' was drawn by the Second Vatican Council's missionary decree.

> So too, indeed, just as happened in the economy of the
> incarnation, the young churches, which are rooted in
> Christ and built on the foundations of the apostles, take
> over all the riches of the nations which have been given
> to Christ as an inheritance.[43]

'Incarnation' was used in the decade following the Council as a popular substitute for the less favoured 'adaptation' until it was supplanted by the term 'inculturation'. Indeed, it had much to do with the introduction of the later term. The parallel between Incarnation and missionary evangelization rests on the analogy of Christ's own cultural education at the hands of contemporary Jewish society. It is a parallel that Metz, Calvez and other theologians and missiologists have found wanting.[44] On the positive side, it suggests that Christ himself is the subject of inculturation, that his cultural education was an essential part of his taking human flesh, that he was inserted by the Incarnation into the intercultural dynamic (more immediately Greek, Roman, Hebrew) of human history, and that he needs cultures for the universal spreading of the Good News and the sharing of his life. On the negative side, the parallel plays down the challenge which Christ offered to his own culture and the climax of the whole Christ-event in the Paschal Mystery. It also suggests that the Gospel, like the divine pre-existence of Christ, comes to the evangelized culture in a culturally disembodied form, and that the inculturation process is limited to the Gospel's first insertion in a culture.

For all these reasons, it is theologically more fruitful to draw a parallel between inculturation and the Paschal Mystery, rather than between inculturation and the Incarnation alone.[45] In fact, inculturation is linked causally and analogically to the Paschal Mystery. It is through his passion, death and resurrection that Christ effectively became universal Lord, and that he made himself available in the Spirit to people of every human culture. The Paschal Mystery also offers us an analogy for the conversion or *metanoia* of culture. To become more authentic and more faithful to its underlying truth, a culture must 'die and rise again' under the impact of evangelization, the invitation to respond to Christ's self-gift in history and to become more fully human by adopting the 'Christic model', the pattern of Christ's death and resurrection.[46]

Ecclesiological bases for inculturation

So far, the theological approaches we have considered remain somewhat speculative, but they are useful allies in the debate with culturalists who dispute the relevance of the Christian Gospel to human cultural development. With Amalorpavadass's other two approaches we enter the domain of ecclesiology and even of Church *realpolitik*. The universal mission of the Church is a theme that comprises every aspect of Christianity's lived pluralism. One approach is to see inculturation as a logical consequence of the great commandment of love for God and neighbour. Love, as Pénoukou points out, must take account of human differences.[47] We are called to love others in their difference, in their very otherness. This is the example of Christ, and as Metz demonstrates, it is simply an extension of his preferential option for the poor.[48] The encounter between inculturation theology and the theology of liberation is nowhere more striking than here. This option entails entry into the 'world of the poor'.[49] Sociologists rightly reject the concept of a 'culture of the poor' or a 'culture of poverty', since poverty is a way of life caused by social injustice, not an autonomous system of meanings.[50] Nevertheless, the poor do create their own social mechanisms and subcultures, and frequently the genuine culture to which the poor belong is stigmatized by the non-poor. This is to some extent the problem of rich and poor nations today, of Euro-American world culture versus the ethnic traditions of the 'two-thirds world'. Inculturation involves, in practice – and not merely in theory – the recognition of cultural equality, and the human right to culture. In other words, it is pledged to a genuine liberation of culture.

The lived plurality which confronts the Church is not confined to national and ethnic cultures, but includes other cultures or subcultures, such as those of women, youth and adepts of non-Catholic Christian and non-Christian religious traditions. Catholicity, therefore, implies an experiential and ecumenical dynamic, a true communication of meaning. Since language is closely tied to culture, the meeting with others in their otherness demands a sensitivity to language. The language of faith can be no other than the language of the evangelized culture. There can be no universal or standardized language in a truly Catholic Church.

This realization raises many questions concerning the role of a centralized *magisterium*, and therefore leads into the final theological starting-point for inculturation, which is that of the Church's authentic tradition and its ordinary *magisterium*. Speaking of the particular Churches, the Second Vatican Council's dogmatic constitution on the Church stated:

> It is in these and formed out of them (*in quibus et ex quibus*) that the one and unique Catholic Church exists.[51]

It fell to those who drafted the Council's missionary decree to spell out in greater detail the shape of the particular Church, the main activity of which is to reconcile local culture with the Church's universal tradition.[52] The questions have then to be asked: What is the substance of this universal tradition? Has it any cultural significance?

The Church's universal tradition is centred on the place of Jesus Christ in human history and on the interpretation of the Christ-event. That interpretation is conceived by Raymond Brown as a 'trajectory' of meaning or 'doctrinal trajectory', which goes back to New Testament outlooks and within which further interpretation takes place, as 'The tradition which comes from the apostles makes progress in the Church, with the help of the Holy Spirit'.[53] Being a living thing and a historical phenomenon, the Church's tradition constitutes a growth of insight and even the acquisition of surplus meaning.[54] We actually participate in the revealing process.[55] Sacred tradition, therefore, passes from 'culture to culture', from 'history to history' and from 'clarity to clarity', as it moves organically from one inculturation to another or as contemporaneous inculturations interact within the universal communion of the Church.[56]

To grasp these developing insights and to make them fruitful in the life of the Church, it is necessary to decode the faith-statements of other ages and places and to reformulate and live them in the cultural language of our own faith.[57] This procedure is strictly necessary if we take the Church's dogmas seriously, and it immediately relativizes their cultural significance. Amalorpavadass makes the further point that we often speak of the Church's tradition as if, until now, it was always couched in the forms of a single, Western or Euro-American culture. The reality is that, in spite of apparent Western dominance, the Church's tradition is culturally pluriform.[58] The imperialism of a single Christian culture in the Church contradicts its vocation of Catholicity.

The history of the Church, however, is the history of an intercultural process (acculturation), and this means that syncretism is always with us. Not only do elements from a Christian evangelizer culture enter into the final Christian synthesis of an evangelized culture when evangelization takes place, but a currency of more or less contingent cultural elements of diverse origin accumulates and is passed from one inculturated form of Christianity to another. This is what I have ventured to call the 'cultural patrimony' of the Church.[59] This patrimony certainly does not constitute a culture in the accepted sense of the term, and it should not be allowed to become what it frequently threatens to be – a Catholic world subculture. It is a syncretic component of inculturation, and there is a tolerance level for syncretism which it is dangerous to exceed. It must certainly never be confused with the tradition of faith.

Evangelization and dialogue

Inculturation has been described as the ongoing dialogue between culture and religious faith. In fact, religion is by definition a cultural system.[60] It helps people construct their lives, using the symbols and concepts of their culture. Social anthropologists usually identify a variety of levels within a given culture. The more superficial levels relate to the technology of the workplace or the home. However, there are deeper levels of life-choices, values and beliefs. The deepest cultural level relates to an understanding of humanity and its place in the world. This level is explicitly or implicitly religious; that is to say, it indicates a consciousness of superior power that transcends sense experience.[61] Of course, there are people who remain content to locate their cultural absolute at the technical level. This, by and large, is what considerable numbers of people do in secular Europe and North America. However, in so far as people are religious, they enter into the deeper levels of culture, and, according to the religion they profess, conduct a necessary dialogue with them.

All of this means that evangelization/inculturation frequently involves interreligious or inter-faith dialogue. This has been defined as 'all positive and constructive interreligious relations with individuals and communities of other faiths, which are directed at mutual understanding and enrichment'.[62] Dialogue has sometimes been mistakenly opposed to evangelization, as if the Church should replace preaching of the Gospel and conversion work by an open-ended encounter with other faiths. Some have even gone so far as to claim that interreligious dialogue is now the only legitimate activity for evangelizers, suggesting either that any other strategy implies coercion, or that the resistance of other faiths rules out Christian work for conversion. Against this, it should be noted in passing that the Gospel of Christ can only be accepted in freedom, and that religious freedom is also a fundamental human right.

It is important that, in reacting to this abuse of dialogue, we should not fall into the opposite extreme of subordinating dialogue to proclamation, conversion work and Church implantation. Evangelization and inculturation seek the conversion of peoples and cultures, the permeation of human culture by Gospel values. Dialogue results in a 'conversion' of Christianity. Indeed, it is an essential aim of dialogue that all the parties involved undergo conversion in a wider sense of the word. In dialogue, Christians challenge others and are challenged by them.[63] Let us explore this idea a little more fully.

Professor Frank De Graeve's distinction between 'Christianity' and 'Christ-ianity' is helpful here.[64] 'Christianity', according to this distinction, stands for the Church and the Gospel as we know them here and now. They represent the historical tradition of faith to which we proclaim our present allegiance. This is the tradition which we invite others to share by accepting baptism into the communion of the Church. However, although the Church is really Christ's Body, and although he is already really incarnate in its varied cultural forms, he is not yet exhaustively present. He still transcends the Church, and we await the *pleroma* of God, the full adulthood of Christ or eschatological fullness of his presence, when God will be 'all in all' (Ephesians 1:23).

This *pleroma* of God is what De Graeve means by 'Christ-ianity'. The non-Christian religions do not find their ultimate fulfilment in a given form of historical Christianity, but in their consummation in Christ. The reality of Christ comes to a larger self-understanding through its discovery in different traditions. This is the revelation of 'Christ-ness' in all religion. Each religion, including historical Christianity, must be brought by the Spirit of Christ to perfection through sharing, through self-purification and growth. This is the conversion to which the Church is also called through dialogue. Pope John Paul II has described the process of continual conversion very movingly.

> Authentic knowledge of the God of mercy, the God of tender love, is a constant and inexhaustible source of

39

conversion, not only as a momentary interior act but also as a permanent state of mind. Those who come to know God in this way, who 'see' him in this way, can live only in a state of being continually converted to him. They live, therefore, *in statu conversionis*; and it is this state of conversion which marks out the most profound element of the pilgrimage of every man and woman on earth *in statu viatoris*.[65]

Because the Church lives in a state of continual conversion, it welcomes dialogue with other religions. It is through dialogue that our understanding of the Christian faith develops, new insights are learned, and new discoveries are made. The tradition that comes from the apostles 'makes progress in the Church', which itself advances 'towards the plenitude of divine truth'.[66] It is through dialogue that the historical Church is able to assume new cultural forms (inculturation) and be the instrument through which existing cultures are evangelized. The Church and other religions become more what they truly are, by growing closer together in dialogue.

Dialogue is integral to evangelization, and can be said to qualify proclamation, because it takes its origin in the nature of the Blessed Trinity. We are reminded of this by the Pontifical Council for Interreligious Dialogue:

> God is love (1 John 4:8, 16). This saving love of God has been revealed and communicated to mankind in Christ and is present and active throughout the world by means of the Holy Spirit. The church is the living sign of that love in such a way as to render it the norm of life for all. This mission, Christ's own, is one of love because in him it finds its source, goal and way of proceeding (cf. *Ad Gentes*, 2, 5, 12; *Evangelii Nuntiandi*, 26). Each aspect and activity of the church's mission must therefore be imbued with the spirit of love if it is to be faithful to Christ who commanded the mission and continues to make it possible throughout history.[67]

The Church's prophetical tradition of proclaiming the Good News must be inspired and guided by the Spirit of Love. The great commission and the great commandment are both aspects of evangelization.[68] Indeed, from a historical point of view, we observe the Church growing out of an almost exclusive emphasis on verbal proclamation into a greater insistence on the demands of a universal loving encounter with others. This encounter enables Christians to discern the presence of God in unfamiliar contexts, and provokes an internal dialogue in the heart and conscience of Christians.

It is important to underline, therefore, that the Church does not enter into dialogue for ulterior motives, to annex or take over other religions. The Church undertakes interreligious dialogue in order to be saved, in order to grow in Christ, in order to co-operate with the Holy Spirit at work in other religions. The Church has no monopoly of the process. The Church of today is not the end of the process, and we do not yet know how it will change and develop historically as a result of dialogue. The partners enter into dialogue in strict fidelity to their own traditions, but with a common commitment to a future horizon of truth.

A first prerequisite for dialogue, therefore, is self-identification. One cannot conduct dialogue with other traditions in ignorance of one's own identity. One's own position must be clear. Then there are basically four outcomes of dialogue. Firstly, there is the likely discovery of agreement. Secondly, there is the equally likely area of disagreement, the grounds for which must be diminished as far as fidelity to one's own tradition allows. Thirdly, there is the possibility of a divergence of interests, according to which different religious systems ask different questions of experience and receive different answers. This is the most fruitful area of dialogue, because it is through learning new interests from one another that religious traditions can bring about the fourth outcome, which is convergence.

Another approach to dialogue is offered by Peter Berger.[69] True dialogue excludes 'deduction', the desire to deduce truth exclusively from one's own tradition. It also excludes 'reduction', the desire to reduce the plurality of religions to a meaningless common denominator. It has, instead, to be 'induction', a process by which our own tradition grows by being authentically reinterpreted as a result of the exchange with other traditions. This is another way of saying that dialogue leads to conversion.

As Christians, we cannot speak of God's activity in other religious traditions without reference to Christ as the foundation and norm for the revelation of who God is. We need criteria by which we can identify the action of God. Nothing which comes from God can contradict what we know of him through Jesus Christ. His normativity is being constantly enriched by the Spirit at work in other religions; and it is the Spirit who guides and deepens the process by which God discloses himself in the history and interaction of religions. We do not, therefore, reject other religions as vehicles of salvation-revelation, nor do we abandon the definitive character and particularity of salvation-revelation in Jesus Christ. Instead, we believe that there is a dialectic between

Word and Spirit, and that Jesus has 'many things' yet to say to us through the Spirit who leads us into the fullness of truth about him. Because of this promise, attentiveness to other religious traditions is part of the Church's vocation.

Dialogue and proclamation are both necessary, but how are they related? Dialogue is a relatively new phenomenon in the Church, and it has been accompanied by a lessening of emphasis on unrestrained proselytism, and, indeed, on verbal proclamation. However, proclamation and dialogue do not undermine one another. Dialogue, in some sense of the word, is a necessary prerequisite of proclamation. Without it, faith cannot be deepened or expressed, nor can inculturation take place. On the other hand, an explicit witness to the Gospel – if not proclamation in the strict sense – is also a prerequisite of dialogue, since the Christian interlocutor must carry out a preliminary self-identification, and must continually resort to Christ as the dynamic norm of God's self-revelation in other traditions. Over and above this, however, stands the comprehensive missionary activity of building the Kingdom of God, and of a faith seeking deeper understanding, to which interreligious dialogue intrinsically belongs.

Moreover, dialogue expresses the relational aspect of evangelization, and is indeed its primary mode. As we saw in the first chapter, evangelization is not a mechanistic activity by which a message is transmitted by one set of people to another in an exclusively, or predominantly, verbal manner. Dialogue is primarily experiential. It involves sharing the life, and to some extent the worship, of people in other religious traditions. It also indicates a habit of mind, an openness or flexibility, which is able to interiorize experience and to grow through relationships, rather than to struggle to conform to a static and preconceived model. Ultimately, the notion of dialogue is inherent in the whole history of salvation and in the Incarnation itself. God has revealed himself more clearly and authentically through the providential interaction of human traditions. The First Testament is witness to this. Undoubtedly also, the multicultural character of Palestine in general and Galilee in particular was a providential backdrop for the revelation of the New Testament.

Dialogue may be demanded by the religious and cultural pluralism which confronts us in the contemporary world, but it is far more than a strategy for more effective evangelization. The love, freedom and mutual respect which are intrinsic to dialogue belong to the whole Christian or Gospel way of life, and this, in turn, is the perfection of what it means to be human. Dialogue is, therefore, not an optional luxury for the Church.

Evangelization is characterized by the dialogical qualities of listening and mutual respect. There are four types of dialogue: the witness of a silent presence, theological discussion, spiritual sharing and active collaboration in life situations. The first is a 'silent dialogue' in which people simply share their human problems and preoccupations. It is sometimes called the 'dialogue of life'.[70] The second is the kind of dialogue which most frequently springs to mind when the term is mentioned. The third has come into prominence for Catholics after Pope John Paul II set the example of the multi-faith gathering at Assisi in 1988, and has been repeated many times. But the strongest emphasis should be placed on the fourth, the experiential dialogue or 'dialogue of action', resulting in joint initiatives and practical co-operation.

The dialogue of action is probably the most practical form of dialogue, since it does not require the intimate collaboration of theological élites. It is also a necessary precondition for the efficacy of official, institutional dialogue. Without an interpersonal sharing of lived faith by the adherents of various religions, the agreements of experts cannot be put into effect.

The credibility of evangelization is directly related to ecumenical dialogue between the Christian Churches. Christ's prayer for unity was offered 'so that the world may believe' (John 17:21). However, many Christian denominations, and especially new fundamentalist or independent movements, are far from convinced of the necessity of ecumenism. Some are deliberately divisive, stressing the need for only a faithful remnant to uphold the purity of the Gospel; while others do not believe in the need for any visible or structured communion among groups of Christians. Ecclesiology is as relevant to ecumenism as it is to inculturation; and, without some common assumptions concerning the nature of the Church, interChurch dialogue becomes difficult, if not impossible. An understanding of history is also strictly necessary for ecumenical dialogue, because it determines present-day attitudes. Without it, those who enter into dialogue are walking unsuspectingly over a minefield of differences and difficulties. It is also true that history must be studied before it can be discounted as irrelevant in any given instance.

Dialogue with a world religion: Islam

In many ways the unsystematic nature of Hindu and Buddhist practice renders formal theological dialogue with these world religions difficult. So also does their tendency towards syncretism and inclusivism, at least in their popular forms. In the case of

Islam dialogue is rendered difficult by other factors. One is the different way in which Christianity and Islam have developed historically. Whereas Christians have been constantly challenged by liberal and scientific thought and have developed a critical self-understanding, Muslims are, in practice, unable to take a critical approach to their tradition. Before serious dialogue is possible, Islamic public opinion must allow Muslim scholars to make use of critical exegesis and theology. Another difficulty is that Muslims are not convinced of the need for dialogue with Christians. Their priority is to recover their own Islamic culture after the negative experience of Western colonial rule, and they tend to perceive the pressures of modern technological culture on their religion as part of a Christian–Zionist plot against their religion.

Christians have, to a large extent, accepted dialogue and its consequences. They have largely abandoned conscious and explicit disrespect towards Muslims in their catechesis and publications. The Second Vatican Council asked Christians and Muslims 'to strive sincerely for mutual understanding'.[71] Muslims, on the other hand, continue to pour out anti-Christian propaganda, and to publish material which Christians find hurtful and disrespectful.

Probably the most intractable obstacle to Islamo-Christian dialogue is the fact that Muslims feel they already know the true message of Christ from the Qur'an itself. In fact, the Islamic holy book reproaches Christians for being unfaithful to the teaching of Jesus and for adding secondary beliefs, such as the Trinity, the Incarnation and the Redemption. What the Qur'an says about Jesus is considered to be a dogma which dispenses Muslims from listening to what Christians say about their own faith and tradition. Moreover, Christians and Muslims disagree about the right to freedom of conscience. Whereas Christians respect those of their number who embrace Islam, Muslims often ostracize their co-religionists who become Christians, deny them civil rights and even threaten them with death. Muslims are also more reluctant than Christians to reject proselytism and the exertion of physical and moral pressure on people to convert to Islam. A good example is provided by the Islamic law in black Africa which effectively forbids inter-faith marriages for Muslims.

The problem of religious freedom and reciprocity between Muslims and Christians needs to be addressed. Steps should be taken to see that Christians are better informed about Islam, and a heartfelt appeal must be made to Muslims to live in peace with other religions. Peace demands justice, freedom and mutual respect. It also demands a common faith in God. Jews, Christians and Muslims all have a tradition of faith that goes back to Abraham, the 'father of faith'. There can be no lasting peace between them, if it is not the peace of God himself.

Dialogue with traditional religion

In 1977, I offered myself to the Catholic bishops of an African country to carry out what I called a 'ministry of dialogue with African traditional religion (ATR)'. I explained that I would try to organize formal dialogue with representatives of traditional religion, that I would help Christians in their discernment of religious values in these traditions, and that I would run courses in ATR for priests, religious, seminarians and laity. I made this proposal after organizing the meeting with spokesmen for ATR on behalf of the Pontifical Council for Interreligious Dialogue (then the Secretariat for Non-Christians), which was mentioned earlier in this chapter. My suggestion was not taken up. Instead, I was appointed to teach moral theology in a major seminary. The call for research and dialogue has so far fallen on deaf ears. As long ago as 1966, the document *Ecclesiae Sanctae*, which laid down the norms for implementing the missionary decree *Ad Gentes Divinitus*, called for the setting up of study groups to study traditional religious thought and to undertake theological research.[72] Very little was ever done at the national level. One of the very few countries to take the directive seriously was Tanzania, where I was privileged to belong to the National Committee for Cultural Research, which operated in the late 1970s. In 1988 the Pontifical Council for Interreligious Dialogue issued a letter on 'Pastoral Attention to African Traditional Religion'. This letter concluded with the suggestion that each episcopal conference should appoint a small research group to work with Catholic theological faculties in Africa on the subject of ATR.

Nothing is likely to be done until the authorities are convinced that ATR should be taken seriously. Traditional religion has been despised. Its adherents have been labelled 'pagan', 'heathen', 'idolatrous', 'polytheist', 'primitive', 'primal'. Its beliefs and practices have been represented as an amorphous collection of 'customs' and 'rituals', contrasting unfavourably with the so-called 'higher religions' or 'world religions'. Until comparatively recently, scholars were sceptical about the historical study of African religion and it was the victim of every shade of racial and religious prejudice. Worst of all, ATR was pictured as 'the empire of Satan', rather than as 'Africa's Old Testament' or the 'seed-ground of the eternal Logos'.

A new tactic is to play down the importance of traditional religion. Because many of its visible aspects have disappeared, or are disappearing, it is fashionable to say that ATR itself is part of 'vanishing Africa'. This point of view ignores the important non-visible aspects of tradition, the religious values and beliefs which lie very close to the surface in every human community. And it also takes no account of the fact that traditional religion is acquiring many new external forms, in modern creative writing and myth-making, in new religious movements and even within mainline Christianity.

Traditional religion must be seen as an autonomous religious system apart from and distinct from Christianity. Only then is it possible for the Church to dialogue with it, and for Christians to make the necessary discernment of what is, or is not, compatible with the Gospel. The refusal to take it seriously has bedevilled evangelization and has led to a form of 'split personality' among Christians – an unresolved syncretism which impoverishes both Christianity and tradition, instead of mutually enriching them.

Sects and new religious movements

The two major challenges to the Church are those provided by Christian fundamentalist sects and the Independent Churches. The problem of fundamentalist 'Faith' or 'Bible' movements is a serious one. These movements often preach the imminent end of the world. They are strongly anti-communist and anti-socialist; often they are pro-Israeli and anti-Arab. The fundamentalists teach that material prosperity and physical health are simply a matter of faith and that sin is a private matter. Satan and evil spirits are used to divert people's attention from the real causes of injustice. Christians are told that the world is not their concern, and that obedience to even the most right-wing, totalitarian government is a Christian duty. Finally, they frequently suggest that once a believer possesses the conviction of being saved, it is impossible to fall from grace.

Such ideas are directly opposed to a Catholic understanding of evangelization, but they are already beginning to infiltrate the Catholic Church in some countries. Catholic healing and exorcism movements are beginning to appear, sometimes under the guise of inculturation, and waging war on evil (often Islamic) spirits. African Catholics float between their own parish churches and the massed rallies and meetings of the sects. Alleged Marian apparitions are used in order to discredit Church authority, Church renewal or the concept of a social Gospel. Like their Protestant counterparts, Catholic fundamentalist movements also originate in Western countries: North America, Europe, Australia, and they also propagate the health and wealth syndrome.

Independent Churches are not usually offshoots from missionary Churches in any strict sense. Although a few originated in corporate secession, most are independent in the sense of being independent inventions by prophetic founders. There have been extensive studies of these Churches by scholars and many causes of their appearance have been identified: theological, psychological, social, racial, political. The traditional threefold division of these Independent Churches is still valid: those which are close to mainline Christianity in one or another form; those which are closer to the Hebrew Bible; and those which, in spite of Christian or biblical syncretic components, are closer to traditional religion. Independent Churches are not necessarily homogeneous organizations, even when, as is usually the case, they are ethnically based. There may be a considerable variation in their doctrine and practice, as well as structural proliferation and segmentation. All of this makes dialogue extremely difficult.

Evangelization and liberation

Liberation is a comprehensive concept which is certainly not restricted exclusively to ideas of religious salvation on the one hand, or to those of social justice on the other. We have seen that cultural liberation and the desire to safeguard cultural identity are among the goals of oppressed peoples today. We have also discussed the dialogue of action which can frequently become a force for integral development and socio-economic liberation, and which is itself a dialogue with the concrete circumstances of life.

'The truth will set you free' (John 8:32). This truth is nothing other than the Gospel, the Good News; and this Good News liberates. Basically, the Good News is about the Kingdom of Jesus Christ and his universal lordship. This Kingdom and this universal reign were achieved through his Paschal Mystery: his passion, death and resurrection. The Gospel is ultimately, as Leonardo Boff says, the Good News of the resurrection.[73] There is no better synonym for liberation than resurrection, which means rising to new life. The resurrection enables us to triumph over death and over all forms of diminution of human life. The resurrection constitutes Christ's victory over every form of evil, particularly sin and the suffering caused by sin. Through faith in Christ we join his combat with evil and are given a share in his victory. As a result, we enjoy the freedom of a new life in him, which is the life of his Spirit.

Faith in Christ, then, entails a commitment to the struggle with evil in all its forms. We identify individual sin, particularly in ourselves, but we also identify social sin. This is the outcome of an accumulation of personal sins which affects the structures of society, the philosophies and fashions of our times. As the Bible recounts, sin has grown throughout human history to ever greater proportions. It should not be a surprise for us that we live in an age of moral bankruptcy, of violence, injustice, oppression, corruption and sexual degradation. Christians are engaged in the fight against all of this. Without the certainty of Christ's victory, we would be discouraged, but with that certain knowledge we have nothing to fear. That knowledge brings freedom. It liberates us and empowers us to continue the struggle. We are no longer enslaved by this evil, no longer fettered by fear or weakness.

Above all, faith in the Gospel gives us the freedom to be ourselves. Not only does it help us discover our true nature, but it helps us become what God wants us to be. It enables us to fulfil our true goal in him. This is what genuine religious faith always does. It not only helps people to understand the nature of things, but it gives them the power to construct their lives in accordance with this vision of truth. It is both explanatory and efficacious.

As we saw in Chapter 1, evangelization is productive. It has the power to produce what is proclaimed, and this is one reason why praxis is an integral aspect of evangelization. Basic ecclesial communities are an example of this. They are found not only in Latin America, but also in countries of Africa, Oceania and South East Asia. In these vibrant communities the Word of God is read aloud and is applied, through Bible sharing, to the personal and collective lives of Christians. In this way evangelization opens people's eyes and 'conscientizes' them, to use the term coined by Paulo Freire in Brazil. They discern their own responsibility for the evil within and outside themselves, but they also discern the ways in which evil is structured throughout human society. They go from proximate to remote causes of oppression and injustice. Together they make a common appraisal of the situation, social, political, economic.

Then they pass from knowledge to commitment, from judgement to action. They realize their responsibility to live the Gospel and put it into practice. Proclamation, therefore, leads inexorably to praxis, and basic community members offer to take concrete steps to put right abuses and to bring social reality into line with the Gospel ideal. Much that is achieved by these basic ecclesial communities is accomplished in the immediate life context of their members, but they have also contributed to the democratization of the wider society and to the reaffirmation of human rights and freedoms at the higher social levels. It is often at these levels that the causes of grass roots suffering are to be found.

Basic Christian communities are the classic instance of the powerful being evangelized by the poor, and of God speaking through the mouths of the poor. The Gospel is essentially a call to the non-poor to enter the world of the poor and to discover their values, the principles which unite them by preference to Jesus Christ. There is no doubt that the Gospel constitutes a critique of the rich, of rich individuals, rich nations and rich continents. As Gustavo Gutiérrez explains, it is an answer to the question: 'How do we tell the poor that God loves them?'[74] The answer is that we can only do so through practical deeds of human love. The Gospel is an invitation to conversion, the call to make an option in love for those whom God himself loves. Evangelization, therefore, promotes the freedom which derives from solidarity. This is a word much beloved of Pope John Paul II.

> Solidarity helps us to see the 'other' – whether a person, people or nation – not just as some kind of instrument, with a work capacity and physical strength to be exploited at low cost and then discarded when no longer useful, but as our 'neighbour' to be made a sharer, on a par with ourselves, in the banquet of life to which all are equally invited by God.[75]

Liberation is not, however, measured merely by political change, still less by social revolution, though these may be a result of evangelization as praxis. In fact, there are several recent instances where Christian people-power has played a part in bringing about socio-political change for the better. Such changes, however, are never lasting, and the sinful condition of humanity ensures that the call to liberation and conversion must be a constant one. This is where prayer takes over from proclamation and praxis. Evangelization liberates through prayer and sacramental action. These effect a spiritual liberation in the evangelized. Through prayer and union with God, they enjoy a freedom of heart which is a share in God's own freedom. It is an ability to begin to see the world with God's eyes and to 'think the thoughts of God, not human thoughts' (Matt 16:23). It brings about a liberation from attachments and from prejudices. It turns the believer towards God and towards other human beings. Above all, it creates a yearning for fulfilment which only God can satisfy, and which relativizes all worldly concerns and objectives.

Evangelization/liberation is ultimately prayer, because complete or perfect liberation is not attainable in this life. Prayer points us to the source of ultimate freedom and puts us in touch with him. Obviously, a basic ecclesial community is not merely a prayer group, if only because valid prayer demands active commitment. However, prayer lies at the heart of all true liberation. Not only does it reveal a divine liberator who transcends the limitations of our own lives, times and cultures, but it motivates us to hasten the ultimate liberation through praxis. It does this by imparting an eternal value to our actions in the struggle against evil on earth. In the final analysis, our whole Christian life is supposed to be a prayer, an act of praise and worship of God.

There is no doubt that evangelization encompasses the political, but political liberation is not the final goal of evangelization. Evangelization is necessarily a constant call to an ever more complete liberation. The Gospel love-ethic has inspired many forms of liberation from Wilberforce and Tolstoy to Gandhi and Martin Luther King. It underlies civil rights campaigns and movements for democratization all over the world. It is a new wine calculated to burst old wineskins. This is because the values of the Gospel derive their power from a deep human yearning for total liberation, or more precisely, resurrection. The Truth sets us free, and the Truth offers us all a share in his boundless freedom.

Inculturation, dialogue and liberation are all ways of speaking about evangelization and all ways of experiencing evangelization. Without addressing the human phenomenon of culture, without entering into genuine dialogue, and without being truly liberative, evangelization is not honest or authentic. In the following chapter, we examine the various kinds of evangelization which conform to the different Christian vocations. Especially important is the concept of preaching the Gospel to the unreached nations, or 'primary evangelization', as it is called. In the missionary vocation, the aspects of inculturation, dialogue and liberation appear at their clearest and most demanding. However, the Church's mission is changing, as the cultural configuration of countries and continents changes. There is truth in the saying that, nowadays, mission is where you are. We shall therefore study the changing patterns of missionary work and their relevance for evangelization. After that, in Chapter 4, we shall look at the practical consequences for the Church and for ecclesiology of evangelization seen as inculturation, dialogue and liberation, and we shall study the obstacles which are placed in its path. These obstacles occur both inside and outside the Church, and they are largely bound up with an inherent Western cultural bias.

References

1 Actually, the last two years were spent at Eldoret in Kenya, to which the Gaba Institute moved at the end of 1975.

2 Gerald A. Arbuckle, *Earthing the Gospel* (London: Geoffrey Chapman/ Maryknoll, NY: Orbis Books, 1990), p. 18.

3 K. O. Bimwenyi, 'Inculturation en Afrique et attitude des agents de l'évangélisation', *Bulletin of African Theology*, vol. 5 (1981), pp. 5–17.

4 Leonardo Boff, *New Evangelization* (Maryknoll, NY: Orbis Books, 1991), pp. 99–101.

5 Roy Wagner, *The Invention of Culture* (Chicago: University of Chicago Press, 1981), p. 1.

6 Ibid., pp. 4, 12.

7 Ibid., pp. 53, 154.

8 Cf. Edmond Tang, 'Context and Contextualization', *Pro Mundi Vita Studies*, no. 4 (1988), p. 11; Arbuckle, op. cit., p. 18; P. Schineller, 'Inculturation as the Pilgrimage to Catholicity', *Concilium*, 204 (1989), pp. 98–106; M. L. Stackhouse, 'Contextualization, Contextuality and Contextualism' in Ruy O. Costa, *One Faith – Many Cultures*, (Maryknoll, NY: Orbis Books, 1988), pp. 3–13.

9 B. Lonergan, *Method in Theology* (London: Darton, Longman and Todd, 1973), pp. 301, 326–7; cf. also A. Shorter, *Toward a Theology of Inculturation* (London: Geoffrey Chapman/Maryknoll, NY: Orbis Books, 1988), pp. 17–30.

10 *Evangelii Praecones* in Raymond Hickey, *Modern Missionary Documents and Africa* (Dublin: Dominican Publications, 1982), p. 99, quoting a 1944 address to directors of Pontifical Mission Societies; *Princeps Pastorum*, ibid., p. 143.

11 *Ad Gentes Divinitus*, 10.

12 Ibid., 22.

13 *Gaudium et Spes*, 53.

14 Ibid., 57.

15 Ibid., 58.

16 *Evangelii Nuntiandi*, 63, 20; the latter paragraph cites *Gaudium et Spes*.

17 Cf. Shorter, op. cit., pp. 10, 219, 224.

18 Joseph Masson, 'L'église ouverte sur le monde', *Nouvelle Revue Théologique*, vol. 84 (1962), p. 1038, uses 'inculturation' in adjectival form. This would appear to be the first use of the term, but Charles Chossonnery, 'Toute église est en inculturation permanente', *Bulletin of African Theology*, vol. 6a, no. 11 (1984), p. 134, quotes Meinrad Hebga's assertion that the term was invented by the anthropologist Melville Herskovits in the 1970s. The Federation of Asian Episcopal Conferences spoke of an 'inculturated Church' in 1974; cf. Shorter, op. cit., p. 10.

19 International Theological Commission, 'Faith and Culture', *Omnis Terra*, no. 198 (1989), p. 264; Pedro Arrupe, 'Letter to the Whole Society on Inculturation' in J. Aixala (ed.), *Other Apostolates Today* (St Louis: Institute of Jesuit Sources, 1981), p 172. Aidan Kavanagh, 'L'inculturation de la liturgie: un regard prospectif', *La Maison Dieu*, no. 179 (1989), p. 69, has questioned my use of Arrupe's phrase 'new creation'. It should be obvious, however, that 'creativity' does not preclude the original use of pre-existing sources. If it did, it would, *per impossibile*, lift inculturation out of the intercultural process altogether.

20 W. Reiser, 'Inculturation and Doctrinal Development', *Heythrop Journal*, vol. 22 (1981), pp. 135–48.

21 Michael Amaladoss, 'Dialogue and Inculturation', *Inculturation*, no. 314 (1988), p. 22.

22 Lamin Sanneh, *Translating the Message: The Missionary Impact on Culture* (Maryknoll, NY: Orbis Books, 1990), p. 1; Karl Muller, 'Accommodation and Inculturation in the Papal Documents', *Verbum SVD*, vol. 24 (1983), p. 358.

23 Stackhouse, op. cit., p. 6: Charles H. Kraft, *Christianity in Culture* (Maryknoll, NY: Orbis Books, 1979). These writers use 'context', 'contextuality', 'intercontextuality'. The term 'interculturation' was coined by Bishop Joseph Blomjous in J. Blomjous, 'Development in Mission Thinking and Practice, 1959–1980; Inculturation and Interculturation', *African Ecclesial Review*, vol. 22, no. 6 (1980), pp. 393–8.

24 Shorter, op. cit., p. 224; Stackhouse, op. cit., p. 8; J. M. Waliggo, 'Making a Church That Is Truly African' in J. M. Waliggo *et al.* (eds), *Inculturation, Its Meaning and Urgency* (Nairobi, 1986), pp. 11–30.

25 It can also occur in reverse, when – in the absence of true dialogue – the meaning of another faith is subverted by Christianity. Cf. Wole Soyinka, *Myth, Literature and the African World* (Cambridge: CUP, 1976), pp. 121–2.

26 E. E. Uzukwu, 'Church and Inculturation: A Century of Roman Catholicism in Eastern Nigeria', *SEDOS Bulletin*, vol. 85, no. 10 (1985), pp. 217–22.

27 P. Turner, 'The Wisdom of the Ancestors and the Gospel of Christ: Some Notes on Christian Adaptation in Africa', *Journal of Religion in Africa*, vol. 4 (1971), no. 1, pp. 450–68.

28 William E. Biernatski, 'Some Hard Sayings about Symbolism and Inculturation', *Inculturation*, vol. 3, no. 3 (1988), pp. 20–5; Sanneh, op. cit., p. 91.

29 Robert J. Schreiter, *Constructing Local Theologies* (London: SCM Press, 1985); Adrian Edwards, 'God Above and God Below', *New Blackfriars*, vol. 69, no. 812 (1988), p. 20.

30 Sanneh, op. cit., pp. 37–91.

31 Arbuckle, op. cit., p. 110.

32 John A. Coleman, 'Inculturation and Evangelization in the North American Context', *Proceedings of the Catholic Theological Society of America*, vol. 45 (1990), pp. 15–29.

33 Casimir Guanadickam, 'Inculturation and the Local Church', *Lumen Vitae*, vol. 40, no. 1 (1985), p. 67; D. S. Amalorpavadass, 'Réflexions théologiques sur l'inculturation', *La Maison Dieu*, no. 179 (1989), p. 58; Joseph G. Donders, 'Inculturation and Catholicity in Relation to the Worldwide

Church', *Proceedings of the Catholic Theological Society of America*, vol. 45 (1990) p. 36.

34 L. Newbigin, 'The Enduring Validity of Cross-Cultural Mission', *International Bulletin of Missionary Research*, vol. 12, no. 2 (1988), p. 50.

35 Amalorpavadass, op. cit., p. 61.

36 *Ad Gentes Divinitus*, 11, 22.

37 Shorter, op. cit., p. 197.

38 Shorter, op. cit., pp. 75–8, 121–2, 138–9.

39 John Henry Newman, *Fifteen Sermons Preached Before the University of Oxford* (London: 1909), p. 17.

40 Cf. Sean McDonagh, *To Care for the Earth* (London: Geoffrey Chapman/ Santa Fe: Bear, 1986), pp. 117–21.

41 Ibid., pp. 118, 125–8.

42 Efoé-Julien Pénoukou, *Églises d'Afrique: Propositions Pour l'Avenir* (Paris, 1984).

43 *Ad Gentes Divinitus*, 22.

44 Johan Baptist Metz, 'Unity and Diversity: Problems and Prospects for Inculturation', *Concilium* 204 (1989), p. 81; Jean-Yves Calvez, 'The Real Problem of Inculturation', *Lumen Vitae*, vol. 40 (1985), no. 1, p. 77; Claude Geffré, 'Mission et Inculturation', *Spiritus*, 109 (1987), p. 412; Reiser, op. cit., p. 147; Shorter, op. cit., pp. 81–2.

45 Shorter, op. cit., pp. 83–4.

46 Edmund Hill, 'Christianity and Cultures', *New Blackfriars*, vol. 67, nos 793/ 794 (1986), p. 328; Phil 3:10–11.

47 Pénoukou, op. cit., ch. 1; Shorter, op. cit., p. 78.

48 Metz, op. cit., p. 83.

49 Gustavo Gutiérrez, 'Gutiérrez Speaks to the Missionary Institute London', *MIL Record*, no. 1 (1989), p. 11.

50 J. Gulick, *The Humanity of Cities* (Granby, MA, 1989), pp. 196–200.

51 *Lumen Gentium*, 23.

52 *Ad Gentes Divinitus*, 19–22.

53 Raymond E. Brown, *Biblical Exegesis and Church Doctrine* (New York: Paulist Press/London: Geoffrey Chapman, 1985), p. 28; *Dei Verbum*, 8.

54 Aylward Shorter, *Revelation and Its Interpretation* (London: Geoffrey Chapman, 1983), p. 142.

55 *Catechesi Tradendae*, 35, 37.

56 Cf. Calvez, op. cit., p. 77; F. R. de Gasperis, 'Continuity and Newness in the Faith of the Mother Church of Jerusalem' in P. Beauchamp *et al.* (eds), *Bible and Inculturation* (Rome: Pontifical Gregorian University, Working Papers in Inculturation, 1983), p. 60; Reiser, op. cit., p. 137.

57 Metz, op. cit., p. 86.

58 Amalorpavadass, op. cit., p. 61.

59 Shorter, *Toward a Theology*, op. cit., pp. 65–7.

60 Clifford Geertz, 'Religion as a Cultural System' in M. Banton (ed.), *Anthropological Approaches to the Study of Religion* (ASA Monographs 9; London: Tavistock Publications, 1966), pp. 1–46.

61 Newman, op. cit., p. 17.

62 'Dialogue and Proclamation', *The Bulletin of the Pontifical Council for*

Interreligious Dialogue, no. 77 (1991), vol. 26/2, p. 214, quoting *Acta Apostolicae Sedis*, 76 (1984), no. 3.

63 'Dialogue and Proclamation', 37.
64 Cf. C. Cornille, 'The Eleven Theses of F. De Graeve: A Critical Appraisal' in C. Cornille and V. Neeckebrouck (eds), *A Universal Faith?* (Louvain Theological and Pastoral Monographs, 9; Louvain, 1992), pp. 183–95.
65 *Dives in Misericordia* (Abbots Langley: Catholic Information Services, 1980), p. 67.
66 *Dei Verbum*, 8.
67 'The Attitude of the Church Towards the Followers of Other Religions: Reflections and Orientations on Dialogue and Mission', *Bulletin of the Secretariat for Non-Christians*, vol. 19/2, no. 56 (1984), p. 128.
68 Cf. Francis Cardinal Arinze, 'Dialogue and Proclamation: Two Aspects of the Evangelizing Mission of the Church', *Bulletin of the Pontifical Council for Interreligious Dialogue*, vol. 25/2, no. 77 (1991), pp. 201–3.
69 P. Berger, *The Heretical Imperative* (London: Collins, 1980).
70 'Dialogue and Proclamation', 42.
71 *Nostra Aetate*, 3.
72 *Ecclesiae Sanctae*, 17.
73 Boff, op. cit., pp. 26–7.
74 Gutiérrez, op. cit., p. 11.
75 *Sollicitudo Rei Socialis*, 39.

3   Evangelization and the Christian vocation

Evangelization and Christian initiation

Charles Lavigerie, the nineteenth-century founder of the Missionaries of Africa or White Fathers, advocated the evangelization of
Africans within their own social and cultural milieu. On the one
hand, this strategy entailed the restoration of the catechumenate
of the early Church a century before our own Rite of Christian
Initiation of Adults was introduced. On the other hand, it
demanded the Christianization of indigenous social structures: the
family, the local community and even the chiefdom. Lavigerie
realized that the evangelization of so great a continent could only
ultimately be carried out by the Africans themselves, and he
wanted to make them not only Christians, but apostles. The catechumenate was designed to produce active and committed Christians who had the maturity and self-confidence to spread the
Kingdom of God by themselves.

Lavigerie's strategy was in complete harmony with the nature
of Christian initiation. Baptism makes us members of the faith
community – the Church – and therefore charged with the responsibility of sharing with others our faith in Jesus Christ. In the
sacrament of confirmation this obligation is made even more
explicit. Through it, we are empowered to witness to the Gospel
in our lives, explicitly and implicitly. We become prophets,
endowed with the gifts of the Spirit which embolden us to proclaim the Gospel openly and fearlessly, just as the first apostles
were turned by the Spirit from timid Galilean fisherfolk into
courageous preachers and teachers of the Good News in the urban
centres of the Mediterranean. Every Christian, by virtue of his/
her baptism, is an evangelizer, and the work of evangelization is
bound up with the Christian vocation itself. In fact, it is true
to say that Christian sanctification depends on fidelity to this
apostolate.

It follows that no age is exempt from this responsibility. Not only are active, able-bodied adults expected to be evangelizers, but teenagers and young adults, as well as those entering the 'third age' and those with disabilities. Each one in his/her own life context has the duty of spreading the Kingdom of God. The Christian vocation to evangelize, however, takes various forms and has different emphases. Some of these are more suited to one life context than to another, and we shall discuss these differences later in this chapter.

There is a first point to be made, however, in connection with Christian initiation itself. When people are initiated into the Christian life, they should also be initiated into the task of evangelization. Young people and adults who receive the sacrament of confirmation should be helped to develop an evangelizing role in the community. In some African countries an organization exists called Youth of Light. It is modelled on the successive steps which make up the traditional rites of initiation in Africa.[1] Just as, in the tribe, an individual is brought by degrees to a state of social maturity, so in Youth of Light a young person grows in pastoral responsibility, and this commitment is given an increasing measure of recognition by the whole Christian community. There are also other initiatives in Africa involving young people as evangelizers.

It must be admitted that in traditional, ethnic societies, where considerable emphasis is placed on the wisdom and authority of the elders, people find it difficult to get used to the idea of young people exercising a public role in the community. Young people themselves may also be reluctant to put themselves forward in this way. However, the demography of the African continent demands that the youth play an active social role. Around half the population of Africa is under the age of 21, and this proportion is even greater in the towns and cities. No one nowadays can afford to ignore the younger generation in Africa, least of all the Church. Moreover, the public witness of a teenager or young adult in an African parish community is sufficiently startling to command the attention of older people, as well as of other youngsters.

In European countries, where the average age is growing, and where the over-60s account for considerably more than 20 per cent of the total population, young people appear to feel even more alienated from the Church. In this situation it is imperative that they be actively involved in the Christian community, and that they discover an evangelizing role for themselves. The Taizé community in France has certainly held an appeal for young people all over the world, with its inspiring music, contemplation and community experience, and there are other examples, such as monastic lay communities. Christian student and worker organizations also continue to attract numbers of committed young people. What is needed, however, is a pastoral involvement at the parish level, a form of junior ministry in which young people can evangelize through proclamation, prayer and praxis, and which might become breeding grounds for priestly and religious vocations. Unless imaginative schemes of this kind are introduced, the Church in Europe and the West will become an aging community without a future.

Evangelization, a community responsibility

The activity of evangelization should be an integral part of the life of a baptized Christian, but this does not mean that the evangelizer acts alone. We have already seen that community-building is linked to evangelization; it is also true that evangelization is a community responsibility. Through the sacrament of baptism, a person is inserted into the Christian community and accepts the obligations which this community imposes. We saw in Chapter 1 that the Christian community is both the outcome of evangelization and its driving force. The community is the agent of evangelization and the principal sign of its accomplishment. It is an essential part of the psychology and sociology of religious conversion that a person is attracted to adhere to a community, and that he/she undergoes an exterior change in social behaviour and relationships, as well as an interior transformation.

Religion is by definition a cultural phenomenon, and the Gospel is basically a way of life that is lived in accordance with diverse ⁓ultures.[2] Since culture is always the property of a community and serves to give the community identity, it follows that religious conversion has a community dimension. This is especially true in the case of Christian evangelization, which derives its success and efficacy from interpersonal and community relationships, and which preaches a community ethic based on fraternal love. Christian conversion is therefore never a purely individual and intellectual journey. On the one hand, the community invites the individual to join with it in common witness and worship; and on the other hand, the individual takes the step of joining the community which issues the invitation. The one who responds to the invitation enters into the common field of experience that belongs to this community, adopts its common understandings and judgements, and accepts its common commitments. Even when there is a one-to-one evangelization, the evangelizer acts on behalf of a community and invites the one addressed to join it.

Christian community is, of course, primarily a tangible, local reality. It is not to be identified exclusively with the communion of faith and order which unites all the Church's local manifestations, even though this communion is an indispensable condition for the authenticity of the local Church. Nor is it necessarily the local liturgical assembly, which is often too large and impersonal for real community experience. Community is generally experienced on a smaller scale. The Second Vatican Council teaches that marriage, as a communion of life and love, is the foundation of the family and of the first experience of Christian community.[3] The Council even goes so far as to call the Christian family 'domestic Church'.[4] This idea was developed by Paul VI in the context of evangelization.

> One cannot fail to stress the evangelizing action of the family in the evangelizing apostolate of the laity.
> At different moments in the Church's history and also in the Second Vatican Council, the family has well deserved the beautiful name of 'domestic church'. This means that there should be found in every Christian family the various aspects of the entire Church. Furthermore, the family, like the Church, ought to be a place where the Gospel is transmitted and from which the Gospel radiates.
> In a family which is conscious of this mission, all the members evangelize and are evangelized. The parents not only communicate the Gospel to their children, but from their children they can themselves receive the same Gospel as deeply lived by them.
> And such a family becomes the evangelizer of many other families, and of the neighbourhood of which it forms a part.[5]

It is difficult to exaggerate the importance of the family for evangelization, and, if the family is experiencing a crisis all over the world, then the success of evangelization depends to a great extent on the rehabilitation of the family. The family is under pressure because both parents are out at work, because of a high divorce rate, because of the impact of the mass media, especially television, because of a general breakdown in morality – but most of all because many people who get married want to achieve instant happiness and are not prepared to make the sacrifices on which successful family life is necessarily founded. This attitude is characteristic of the modern 'comfort culture' to which Westerners belong and to which non-Westerners aspire. The solution lies, up to a point, with formal education, with Christian marriage preparation and above all with strong community support for families, which can no longer rely on the backing of a larger circle of relatives.

Where the evangelization of the neighbourhood is concerned, members of a family may join with other Christian families to form small or basic Christian communities, as well as other lay associations and movements. The 1974 Synod of Bishops and Pope Paul VI in *Evangelii Nuntiandi* devoted considerable attention to basic communities.[6] These first appeared in the 1950s in Latin America and in Spanish-speaking countries in other parts of the world. Twenty years later the bishops of East and Central Africa adopted the building of small Christian communities as a pastoral priority. They were followed by other African hierarchies.

Although basic communities were not explicitly mentioned by Pope John Paul II in *Christifideles Laici*, the point was made by him that Church communion can take the form of lay groups, that lay people have the freedom to form such groups and that they need to exhibit certain 'criteria of ecclesiality'.[7] Among these criteria are the need for orthodoxy, for communion with the hierarchy and for fidelity to the Church's apostolate. This agrees with Leonardo Boff's contention that basic communities are in a very real sense 'Church'.[8]

The main purpose of basic or small Christian communities is that they provide an immediate life context within which Christians can practise their faith and carry out their vocation to evangelize. They are a new way of being Church, and of building the Kingdom of God within the neighbourhood. Although Christians join them freely and they reflect given human environments – geographical, socio-economic, interpersonal – small Christian communities help to restructure the parish and to provide a resource for its pastoral team. They are not, therefore, like other lay associations and movements which have an organization that transcends the parish. Small or basic communities exist for the parish and for helping to carry out its evangelizing role.

As a rule, it is easier to build basic communities in rural areas and in urban environments where there is a measure of social cohesion. Very often this means that they flourish mainly among the poor, rather than in the affluent bourgeois climate of suburbia. On the other hand, it is not inconceivable that such communities should be set up among the professional and salaried classes. Very often they may be issue-centred groups of one kind or another. A specialization in the field of social justice, health or the environment need not necessarily militate against a more general pastoral availability, which would place such groups at the service of the parish.

Small Christian communities have many functions. They meet to pray, to study Scripture and to apply it to daily life. They carry out pastoral visits to the sick and needy. They help to organize spiritual retreats and doctrine courses. They intervene to correct abuses of social justice. They offer support to married couples and families. They teach catechism and help to prepare members to receive the sacraments and to celebrate the Sunday liturgy. They contribute to the liturgical and spiritual life of the parish as a whole. They undertake development and co-operative projects. In all these ways small Christian communities carry out the task of evangelization through proclamation, praxis and prayer.

Religious communities are also direct agents of evangelization, as well as models and mentors of basic lay communities. Through their specialized apostolates of teaching, medical care, social work, catechesis and pastoral work, they are immediately involved in the work of proclamation, prayer and praxis, but they also witness to the Kingdom and help to bring it into being through the internal life of their communities. Religious life is at the heart of the Church's mission, which is to evangelize the world. In the following section we shall consider the triple vocation of the Christian and the threefold evangelization to which it gives rise. There is a sense in which all three vocations overlap and are lived by all baptized Christians, whether they are lay people, religious sisters and brothers, or ordained ministers: bishops, priests and deacons. However, they also represent three specializations, which may correspond more closely to the specific charism of a particular religious community.

Evangelization through withdrawal from the world

The triple vocation of the Christian consists in withdrawal from the world, pastoral care and missionary work. Each vocation gives rise to a particular form of evangelization. We consider first the vocation of withdrawal from the world, a vocation which is lived principally by communities of religious contemplatives. At first sight, it might seem strange that withdrawing from the world is compatible with evangelization; however, it is far from being a negative action. On the contrary, withdrawing from it affirms the goodness of the world and its positive values. The world is not rejected as intrinsically evil, but is surrendered as a good, in favour of a higher good. The contemplative withdraws from the world in order to understand it better, and in order to see more clearly the choices and priorities with which the world confronts us.

Whenever I visit a contemplative community, Franciscan, Carmelite, Cistercian, I always notice how interested the members are in the world from which I come. As I sit in the parlour, separated from my interlocutors by a formidable – if largely symbolic – grille, I am astonished that they are able to talk so easily and so knowledgeably about matters which are far removed from their direct everyday experience. Contemplatives may or may not be well informed about life beyond the enclosure, but they display remarkable wisdom and discernment when discussing it. That is, no doubt, why people living in the world choose spiritual guides from contemplative communities. It is also the reason why medieval hermits and anchorites, like Mother Julian of Norwich, exercised so wide an influence beyond the confines of their hermitage. People came from far and near to consult them on every conceivable matter.

The truth is that contemplatives are deeply concerned about the life or death issues which confront people in the world, and they are extremely sensitive to their joys and sufferings. The reason for this is that such things constitute the subject matter of their prayer, and their physical distance from the problems has the consequence of drawing them psychologically nearer to them. Moreover, prayer itself has the effect of shaping attitudes and understandings. 'Love your enemies and pray for those who persecute you', said Jesus (Matt 5:44). Praying for enemies is the best way of changing one's attitude towards them, because prayer teaches us to see people as God sees them and to discover the good which he finds in them. Prayer creates this capacity for deeper understanding.

All of this leads us to an examination of the principal activity of the contemplative, which is prayer. A person withdraws from the world principally in order to pray. In Chapter 1 we touched on the relationship between prayer and evangelization. Basically, prayer helps to achieve evangelization through the communion of saints. The baptized enjoy a communion or fellowship with Christ and with one another, and this fellowship constitutes the Church which is the sacrament of the world, the sign and reality of God's grace in creation. The Church's fellowship is created by the Holy Spirit who renders effective and salutary all that the members do for one another. It follows, therefore, that when the Church prays for its members, when the members pray for the Church, and when the Church's members pray for one another, such prayer is instrumental in realizing God's will for humanity.

God's will for us is primarily focused on the establishment of his Kingdom, therefore prayer helps us to realize that Kingdom and is an effective form of evangelization. Every Christian has a duty of prayer, but for contemplatives, their whole life is centred on the activity of prayer. The contemplative life is not only a reminder to us of this duty; it is also its vicarious fulfilment. It not only convinces us of the importance of prayer in the work of evangelization – that prayer is inseparable from evangelization – it really participates in the redemptive work of Christ building his Kingdom.

Contemplatives participate more obviously and visibly in the activity of evangelization through hospitality, through the liturgical apostolate, through spiritual guidance and through being a school of prayer. Many contemplative communities welcome visitors and guests to their guest wings and retreat houses. Some even have parallel lay communities. The liturgy and the divine office are the official worship of the Church, and contemplative communities carry out this worship with special care and devotion. Visitors are often invited to share this liturgical experience. Contemplatives also create a whole psycho-social and aesthetic context in which visitors and retreatants can discover contemplative prayer for themselves. Through spiritual guidance their members teach outsiders about methods of prayer and help them to develop an authentic prayer life of their own.

Many contemplatives communicate the fruit of their meditation to the world in other ways. They do this, for example, through writing and the print media. Or they may do it through musical composition and music publishing, including the use of electronic media. The monks of Weston Priory in the United States are an outstanding example of a contemplative community with a musical apostolate to the rest of the Church, but there are many others.

Monastic hospitality is often directed primarily to the poor and disadvantaged. Contemplatives may run hospices for the homeless, and provide food for the people of the road. The kindness they show to all comers is a direct witness to Gospel values, and, beyond a doubt, helps to build up God's Kingdom. One of the paradoxes of the vocation of withdrawal from the world is that it acts as a magnet for people in the world. This is exactly what one would expect, since it is essentially a sign and an instance of God's Kingdom.

Pastoral evangelization

By pastoral evangelization is meant the activity of establishing God's Kingdom in the home community. This is the usual form taken by evangelization, the form which concerns the majority of Christians. It is an active form of evangelization in the sense that contemplative prayer is not its principal preoccupation. It is more concerned with proclamation and praxis. It is directed towards the home community. This means a community that is more or less homogeneous and well integrated. Even if it is made up of people of different races and cultures, it supposes that these different groups are in communication with one another. A multicultural community may be a configuration of equally respected participant cultures, or it may consist of a dominant culture with a number of subcultures or infracultures. In any case, what is envisaged in this form of evangelization is a community which is not divided by human barriers and cultural allegiances that prevent normal communication.

Pastoral evangelization is often simply called 'pastoral care'. This does not necessarily denote a passive maintenance of the *status quo*. It may refer to a genuine Church-founding situation. What defines this vocation is not whether the Church has been fully implanted or not, but the fact that the evangelizers are not foreign to the community. On the contrary, they belong to it, either because it is their own local community of origin, or because it is a community of their own nationality and/or culture. This usually implies that the Church has already come into existence in this community. In any case, even if the Church is already well established in this community, it needs to grow both intensively and extensively. The faith of the community needs to be deepened and to find new areas of active application. Different subcultures need to be more fully integrated. Perhaps the dominant culture needs to be challenged. Backsliders have to be drawn back into the community, and new members recruited. Above all, the Gospel must be lived in the real life contexts of the local community, and must address all its genuine interests and concerns. All of this is evangelization in the strict sense – the building of God's Kingdom, through proclamation, prayer and praxis.

Although prayer does not play the same role in pastoral evangelization as it does in the contemplative vocation, prayer – especially liturgical prayer – remains basic. The Good News of the Kingdom is proclaimed and celebrated in the liturgical assembly, in the Eucharist and in the other sacraments. The liturgy helps to weld the community together. It marries people's daily concerns and problems with God's plan of salvation for them. Above all, it nourishes the Church by means of the Holy Spirit, turning it ever more completely and perfectly into the Body of Christ, and helping it reach the completed stature of the Whole Christ. The sacraments bring about the union with Christ which transforms us and makes us subjects of his Kingdom. The liturgy, as we saw in the first chapter, is also an important vehicle of catechesis, of reading

and expounding the Word of God. Pastoral evangelization, therefore, gives an honoured place to liturgical celebration.

In the final analysis, pastoral evangelization means helping
people discover and respond to Christ in their lives. This means
reaching out to them in the places where they live, work and play.
Preaching, teaching and offering spiritual advice at worship centres
have their importance, but organizing pastoral teams, carrying out
pastoral visitation, setting up contact structures, starting associations and founding basic communities may be ultimately more
effective.

Pastoral evangelization requires constant reflection and social
analysis, because the human phenomenon is always changing.
Such analysis helps to identify the various human contexts which
make up the community and which must be addressed by the
Gospel. These contexts undergo change, disappear or come into
fresh existence, as the case may be. To remain pastorally static is
to risk being ineffective and even irrelevant. The pastoral worker
needs to be as well informed as possible, and to be able to read
the signs of the time and interpret them in the light of the Gospel.[9]

Social analysis also reveals those human contexts which are as
yet unevangelized and which are likely to be receptive to the
Gospel. These may be minority groups or categories that are
imperfectly assimilated. They may be age groups that are yearning
for some kind of religious fulfilment. They may also be social
strata deeply affected by justice and peace issues or environmental
concerns. Or else they may be young people at one or another
level of education, learning about life and/or committed to cultural
or sporting activities. The sick, the bereaved, the unemployed,
those convicted of crime are among the many categories of people
who may be willing to consider the relevance of religious faith to
their own situation.

Pastoral evangelization is carried out by ordained ministers
whose task it is to establish and develop the ecclesial community,
and also by pastoral workers who are lay ministers.[10] It should
not be surprising that there is a certain overlap between them,
since the whole Christian community has the responsibility of
pastoral care and of participating in the public worship of the
Church.[11] It is even recommended that priests and pastoral workers
co-operate closely, preferably through teams. Lay ministers include
acolytes and readers at Mass and other roles foreseen by Canon
Law, e.g. baptism, the distribution of holy communion (Eucharistic
ministers) and presiding at prayers.[12] Pastoral workers are also
engaged in the transmission of the faith through catechesis and
preparation for the sacraments, through marriage preparation

and counselling, and especially through parent formation for the Christian upbringing of children.

In many countries of the non-Western world the catechist is not only a catechism or religion teacher, but a lay pastor who leads a village community in Sunday worship, who carries out pastoral visitation, who baptizes in danger of death and who presides at funerals in the absence of the priest. The catechist may also represent his/her community at meetings of the parish pastoral council.

All Christians, whether or not they exercise a lay ministry, are called upon to evangelize their own field of work. Such fields include: industry, commerce, politics, economics, finance, law, medicine, education, sciences, arts and mass media.[13] By and large it is true to say that Christians are not used to applying Gospel principles in these areas. This is because they live in a secular society which tends not to acknowledge such values, and because religion is commonly perceived as being a purely private affair. With the development of Christian ethics and its application to such fields as politics, business and the media, Christians are beginning to realize the relevance of the Gospel to such areas of life. Pastoral evangelization needs to help develop an awareness of Christian ethics and social teaching, so that the Gospel may be proclaimed and lived in every context of work and life. All that lay people do, even as lay ministers or pastoral workers, they do in virtue of the sacraments of baptism, confirmation and, in many cases, matrimony, which they have received.

Pastoral evangelization involves dialogue with many different traditions and 'worlds'. There is a dialogue with the reigning socio-cultural ethos or philosophy of life. In Euro-America, and sometimes elsewhere, this is materialist and secularized. We shall discuss this particular field of dialogue later in this chapter. There is also dialogue with various subcultures, such as those of women and of youth.[14] Ecumenical and interreligious dialogue are also important, particularly nowadays with new religious movements and cults. There is also the dialogue with non-believers – atheists and agnostics. A particular obligation is to identify and dialogue with the world of the poor. Usually the poor are the socially disadvantaged, the casualties of a socio-economic system, the homeless, the disabled. Dialogue can take many forms, but it is a necessary aspect of pastoral evangelization.

From the foregoing discussion it can be seen that pastoral care is very far from being simply a holding operation. On the contrary, it is an active, forward-looking undertaking, which continually strives to build up the Kingdom of God and to make it grow. There is no room for complacency, or for the notion that any community can be definitively Christianized. Human communities are not static entities, but are always fit subjects for evangelization. Moreover, it is a fundamental mistake to think that the Gospel can be domesticated. On the contrary, the Gospel is a never-ending challenge to a changing situation.

Pastoral evangelization implies a commitment to continuous conversion, even to refounding the Church in a situation of radical change.[15] Human societies are subject to regular internal change over long periods of time. In fact, as John Henry Newman remarked, 'To live is to change, and to be perfect is to have changed often'! However, there is also a radical type of change, which involves the replacement of socio-cultural structures. Society and culture are made up of clusters of related social facts, and these clusters are identified by people in the light of accepted theories or models. These we call 'structures'. Thus a cluster which includes rituals of courtship, marriage and childbirth, relationships between spouses, parents and children, as well as between in-laws and other relatives, might be explained in virtue of a given model of the family. When the current family model is abandoned, there is a situation of radical or structural change.

Radical change occurs firstly in the mind. That is why it is so far-reaching. We live today in a world in which not only is change itself radical, but the pace of radical change is accelerated. That is why the Church is in constant need of refounding. We need a Church that is alive, a Church that is on the move.[16] We need great courage, hope and imagination, if we are constantly to refound the Church in a chaotic world. We also need to be committed to living the great commandment of love through the experience of community. Pastoral evangelization is therefore a commitment to refounding the Church and to constant community-building.

An important truth, which has been realized more fully since the Second Vatican Council, is that pastors themselves cannot be simply and totally distinguished from the flock. Clerics, religious and other office-holders in the Church are all part of the people of God and, as such, proper objects of pastoral care. 'Who cares for the carers?' is a question that is often asked. It is being answered by new forms of ministry, by counselling, by courses of pastoral and personal renewal and by spiritual centres. Pastoral evangelization is a work of partnership, in which the partners act and react upon each other. Each needs the help of the other to experience communion in the Kingdom of God's love.

Missionary evangelization

Like pastoral evangelization, missionary evangelization is defined with reference to the vocation of the evangelizer. Whereas, in pastoral evangelization, the evangelizer builds God's Kingdom in his/her own community, culture or local Church, missionary evangelization occurs when the evangelizer crosses a human frontier to build the Kingdom in another culture, another language, another nation or local Church. A frontier or border is both an obstacle and a challenge.[17] It offers a fresh opportunity, an unknown territory to explore, a new adventure. However, it is also a barrier to surmount, a door to unlock, a boundary to cross.

There is a widespread modern illusion that we can live without borders to divide us. There is optimistic talk of a 'universal form of culture' or of a 'global village'.[18] Intense efforts have been made between nations and Churches to eliminate barriers and to create new communities and communions, but not only have the barriers remained, in some cases they have reappeared or been strengthened. It is clear that we cannot live without borders and should not wish to do so. Some borders are given, because they are part of the human phenomenon. They define differences of sex, culture, language, ethnicity, religious experience. Other borders have been created by human beings, and in many cases these are the consequence of perversity and injustice. Such, for example, are the discriminatory barriers between classes and castes, between races, and between rich and poor. Sometimes the man-made barriers reinforce given cultural or ethnic differences.

It is obvious that such frontiers or borders are not defined by geographical distance alone. From whatever vantage point one takes, they can be found both locally and globally. Missionaries, therefore, are not always 'foreign missionaries'. They may travel a great distance to a remote country where the language and culture are similar to those of their country of origin. One thinks, for example, of a British or Irish missionary in New Zealand or Australia. On the other hand, they may travel a short distance to another part of their own home town in order to evangelize a community whose language and culture are very different from their own. For example, a British or Irish missionary might evangelize a Japanese-speaking community in London, or a Bantu-speaking Tanzanian missionary might evangelize a Nilotic- or Cushitic-speaking community in his own country. In such cases, however, the psychological and social distance travelled by the missionary may be greater than the geographical distance.

This complexity of mission contexts is brought about by the

multicultural character of many countries. In Europe and North America this is a relatively recent phenomenon brought about by population mobility and modern means of communication and travel. In many parts of the non-Western world the cultural configuration, which was already complex, was rendered more acute by the creation of new multicultural nation-states. In addition to this, the mission-sending countries of the old Christian West have experienced a massive loss of faith and an overwhelming growth of secularism, while the majority of Christians now belong to the so-called 'young' Churches of the non-Western world which possess an active and vibrant faith. It is not surprising, therefore, that many missionary organizations are now ready to recognize genuine mission contexts in Europe and North America.

Thomas Kuhn identified a succession of paradigms in the history of science. These were sets of recurrent or standard illustrations and applications of theories – a cluster of solved problems and techniques – accepted as the norm by a scientific community.[19] In each case the number of anomalies built up until the reigning paradigm had to be abandoned, and another one adopted. Such paradigm shifts were often painful, and could even be resisted for some length of time, but in the end the new norm came to be accepted. The history of science is thus very far from being a unilinear evolution. Rather it is a succession of tradition-bound periods, broken by revolutions.

Kuhn knew that his theory possessed a wide applicability to other fields, and was even drawn from them. In the late 1980s the Swiss theologian Hans Küng began to apply Kuhn's notion of paradigm to developments in theology. More recently, the missiologist, the late David Bosch of South Africa, has applied it to mission theology.[20] In the Catholic Church we are clearly witnessing a current shift from one paradigm of mission to another. As a result, we are also experiencing the crisis that occurs when the transition to a new paradigm takes place, and when many in the Church continue to cling to the outmoded paradigm. This is very well illustrated by the papal encyclical *Redemptoris Missio* of 1990.

Redemptoris Missio was written to lend support to the Church's missionary activity and to stress that it is a permanent obligation. It was also issued in conjunction with the Decade of Evangelization, to remind Christians that there is a growing number of people in the world who have not yet heard Christ's message. The finest and most theological passages of the encyclical are to be found in the first three chapters, which deal with the mission of Christ, the Kingdom and the role of the Holy Spirit, and it is there that the Johannine mandate to offer people a share in the communion of the Godhead is mentioned.[21] However, the document as a whole stresses the prophetic role of the Church, rather than its sacramental tradition, and places a strong emphasis on proclamation. It attempts unsuccessfully to apply the mission paradigm of the late nineteenth/early twentieth century to a Church and a world that have changed radically, but what gives the document its credibility is the fact that it is aware of the anomalies in the moribund model to which it clings.

The obsolete paradigm stems from the great missionary movement which preceded and accompanied the colonial expansion of Europe. It presents a Eurocentric model, in which the Church in Europe is described as stable, mature and mission-sending, and in which European culture is seen as profoundly Christian. In this situation of ecclesial stability and maturity the evangelizing activity is one of pastoral care. The mission is directed to individuals who belong to the pagan nations of the non-Western world, whose culture is unaffected by Gospel values, and among whom the Church has not yet been firmly planted. Such nations are viewed as passive recipients of the Christian message and passive consumers of European 'Christian' culture. They are not entitled to become mission-sending, because they are still under the tutelage of the Christian West. According to this paradigm, missionaries are sent forth by centralized missionary organizations, controlled by the Roman Curia, on behalf of the universal Church.

The Missionary Decree of the Second Vatican Council, *Ad Gentes Divinitus*, basically adopts this paradigm, although it strives to reconcile it with an admission of cultural pluralism and with the reinstatement (by *Lumen Gentium*) of the local Church as the primary ecclesial reality. However, it was unwilling to recognize mission contexts in the secularized West, because the Church had already been implanted there. *Ad Gentes Divinitus* contained the seeds of a new mission paradigm and of the dynamic concept of 'incarnation', later to be called inculturation.

The new mission paradigm offers the model of a *koinonia* Church, in which local Churches are responsible for mission-sending and reach out to help one another in a variety of needs. Some of these needs involve the practice of pastoral care, and others involve the primary evangelization of non-Christians, as well as the Christian penetration of specialized 'worlds' or levels of human activity. Missionary vocations are recognized wherever they occur, without reference to any standard of ecclesial maturity. In the new paradigm there are no geographically, or even demographically, defined mission territories. Mission takes place wherever a Christian crosses a human frontier to supply a felt need, in accordance with the priorities of the local Church, and this includes Europe and North America.

In the new paradigm, missionary activity is multidirectional and there is a growing interdependence or partnership among local Churches. This relationship is guaranteed and served by the centralized organs of the Church. Missionary activity is dialogical, encountering other cultures and other religious traditions in which the Spirit of God is active. The missionary collaborates with the Spirit in helping the evangelized give a new and creative expression to the Christian mystery, especially in the basic communities, and also in reflecting on the encounter with other faiths. The paradigm envisages an egalitarian world communion of mutually respected local Churches, serving and enriching one another.[22] It is a paradigm which can already be verified. Already it is reflected in the pattern of missionary recruitment and in the identification of mission contexts. The recently founded local Churches of the non-Western world are already sending missionaries and founding missionary societies. Non-Western Christians already outnumber those of the West. Euro-America now hosts a multiplicity of exotic cultures, ethnic groups and non-Christian religious traditions, as well as experiencing a massive loss of Christian faith and a crisis in vocations to the priesthood and religious life.

Redemptoris Missio tries unsuccessfully to correct the anomalies of the old paradigm by inserting selected elements from the new one. It offers the classic hierarchical pyramid when it speaks of missionary leadership.[23] However, the document also speaks about a 'mutual ministry' among the local Churches and affirms that responsibility for missionary activity rests with them.[24] It speaks of mature Churches sending missionaries, but admits that this maturity is not an essential criterion for a missionary vocation.[25] It attempts to define missionary evangelization objectively, in accordance with specific types of activity, especially primary evangelization, and it tries to distinguish between Christian countries and geographically defined missions. However, it frankly admits that such distinctions are now difficult to apply in practice.[26] Europe and North America are said to need a new evangelization, but they are not mission territories and their cultures are still deemed to be Christian.[27] The encyclical adopts a basically exclusivist approach to other religious traditions, and condemns the relativist ideas of certain nameless theologians.[28] However, it admits the provisional nature of the historic Church, and the salvific possibilities of other faiths, and it concedes that interreligious dialogue is 'a healthy challenge' that brings an 'inner purification and conversion'.[29] Finally, the encyclical warns against the dangers of syncretism, implies that the Church is extrinsic to (sinful) human cultures and even describes inculturation as 'translation', while at the same time emphasizing its importance and urgency.[30]

The tension between old and new mission paradigms revealed in the missionary encyclical *Redemptoris Missio* discloses the extent to which Christians, and especially Christian authorities, are reluctant to accept a changed situation. Yet, there is no doubt that a new order is coming into existence and a new understanding of the Church's mission, even if the old paradigm lingers on in its obvious death throes. This certainty, as well as the relevance of the new paradigm to contemporary realities, justifies the definition of missionary evangelization that is given here.

Missionaries are those who cross human frontiers. They are 'frontiersmen' and 'frontierswomen' in other ways also. They are at the frontier of the Church's historical development, pointing to the new forms which the Church is taking, as a result of the dialogue with other faiths and cultures and as a result of the unique experiences and insights of new faith-communities. They – more than other Christians – are attentive to what the Spirit is saying and doing in other religions and traditions. In the universal Church they are the voice of the periphery, of the poor and marginalized, of the so-called 'young' Churches so frequently ignored or disdained by those who consider themselves mature.

Confronted by new and unfamiliar situations, missionaries understand the necessity for socio-religious analysis and anthropological research. They are often the first to become aware of structural injustice and the denial of human rights, and they are the first to suffer – usually by deportation – for drawing attention to such abuses. As the whole world becomes progressively urbanized, missionaries are reflecting on the pastoral challenges offered by the growth and multiplication of towns and cities. This is especially the case in the non-Western world, where the majority of town dwellers suffer inhuman living conditions in shanty-towns and squatter areas. Missionaries are working with these squatters and with all the social and moral casualties of urbanization. In recent years they have become deeply involved in helping non-Western communities cope with the AIDS pandemic and its victims.

The missionary encyclical made scant reference to ecumenism.[31] It conveyed the impression that the main advantage of ecumenical dialogue with Christians of other Churches lay in stemming the rise of fundamentalist sects. No doubt the growth of a form of Christianity which promises instant material rewards for faith, which offers diabolical explanations for social ills and which depoliticizes the poor in the face of their oppressive rulers, is to be resisted. However, the recognition of a common enemy is not the only reason for promoting ecumenism, and most Catholic missionaries are convinced of the movement's intrinsic importance. There is an intimate connection between the missionary vocation and promoting the unity of the Christian faith. Early missionaries competed openly with their rivals for the allegiance of the 'pagans', but this lamentable policy is no longer a luxury to be enjoyed. The Churches are thrown together as never before, particularly in the vast conurbations of the non-Western world. In such places the unhappy religious conflicts of faraway times and countries appear irrelevant, but unity is an urgent necessity if missionaries are to realize Christ's priestly prayer at the Last Supper: 'May they be one, so that the world will believe that you sent me' (John 17:21). A missionary cannot afford not to be an ecumenist.

Formation of the missionary evangelizer

Just as there are ordained and lay pastoral workers, so there are ordained and lay missionaries. In the old paradigm of mission little notice was taken of the lay missionary. It was a clerical paradigm centred on Church planting and on community-building through word and sacrament. Little attention was paid to the immense contribution made by lay people to the work of missionary evangelization, especially by lay catechists, teachers, prayer leaders, development workers and medical personnel. If missionary evangelization is essentially a shared revelation of the Kingdom across human frontiers, and taking place through relationships of love and service, then the laity have an indispensable role. In the new mission paradigm they have the special task of helping to develop a responsible laity in the newly planted Church, and of ensuring that it is a communities-based Church served by lay ministries.

The mission encyclical *Redemptoris Missio* invites further reflection on the missionary role of the laity – largely by its silence on the question. Lay people are required to pray for the missions, look for missionary vocations and give money. Apart from these things, the document sheds little light on how, if at all, the laity are to follow a missionary vocation. We have already admitted that there is an overlap between the contemplative, pastoral and missionary vocations, and it is certainly true that all Christians, in virtue of their baptism and confirmation, are missionary. At the very least, this means that they share a real concern for spreading the Good News of the Kingdom beyond the borders of their own home community, that they are ready to be informed about the Church's missionary activity and to assist it in whatever way they can. Such a commitment is made more urgent by the growing number of multicultural and multi-faith situations, and therefore of local mission contexts.

However, some lay people are called to become missionary evangelizers, local or global, in the strict sense of the word. They really share in the vocation to witness the Gospel across cultural and other human frontiers. They do this, either as pastoral workers, or by pursuing their own specializations and professions. Sometimes they join missionary organizations, either lay missionary movements, or clerical and religious institutes which offer associate status to lay people. More often, they operate as individual professionals in secular structures. In most cases, even if their commitment is not lifelong, they make considerable sacrifices where salaries, job prospects and living conditions are concerned.

One of the most glaring gaps in the missionary encyclical *Redemptoris Missio* concerns missionary formation. It asks that missionaries be given 'a doctrinal and apostolic formation abreast of the times', and stresses their need for 'a new ardour of holiness'.[32] All of this is excellent as far as it goes, but nothing is said about the need for specialist training, especially missiology, sociocultural anthropology, the science of religions and cross-cultural theology. Most of my missionary life has been spent in the formation of missionaries and African clergy, and my experience has convinced me that such professional training is strictly necessary for missionaries. It cannot be assumed that ordinary seminary training or apostolic formation in the home Church, without a mission focus, equips a Christian to cross a cultural frontier and become a missionary evangelizer. Such an assumption leads to discouragement and failure, if not to disaster. It is another assumption that is based on the old Eurocentric paradigm.

In 1968, after university studies and field research in social anthropology, I began lecturing at Gaba Pastoral Institute in Uganda. My pastoral experience was limited and my approach was too academic. However, little by little, I came to identify the pastoral needs of my students and to respond to them. I named my lecture course 'Pastoral Anthropology' and I set out to introduce my mature students to social anthropology and to discuss with them its various practical applications to pastoral work.[33] We examined the relevance of the discipline for Christian moral discernment, for religious education and for the liturgy. Workshops were set up to study the themes and values of African traditional prayer literature and of modern African creative writing, and to create inculturated texts for the Eucharist and other sacramental rites.

As I became more confident, I also encouraged my students,

most of them priests and sisters with some mission experience, to go in for the limited comparative analysis of religious systems and for historical approaches to African traditional religion.[34] I also added topics of special interest to them – community, friendship and ministry – to my basic course. There was little or no opportunity for fieldwork during a nine-month course, but I supervised those who were able to do it. Since I was also in charge of an international research office which undertook a number of research projects for the bishops of eastern Africa, my teaching benefited from my ongoing contacts with the field.

In 1978, I was appointed to Kipalapala Senior Seminary near Tabora in Tanzania. For three years, I taught African theology there, another name for special moral theology. I also taught social anthropology, African traditional religion and homiletics. Although I had no university training in moral theology, I was able to present the African socio-cultural realities, particularly with regard to marriage, family life, social justice and the virtue of religion. The seminarians had a long inter-semester vacation during which I encouraged them to carry out fieldwork of their own. During this time I also served on the Tanzanian national committee for liturgical research and helped to co-ordinate the fieldwork of its members in their study of traditional rituals as a resource for the Christian liturgy.

On leaving Kipalapala in 1980, I was commissioned to carry out a study of urban apostolates in Kenya and Tanzania. I continued with this project after joining the Catholic Higher Institute of Eastern Africa in 1984.[35] At the institute, my students were priests and sisters preparing for advanced degrees in theology. The lecture courses I gave were on specially selected anthropological topics, but most of my energies were directed towards supervising students preparing the ethnographic sections of their dissertations, usually with some fieldwork. More helpful, from a practical point of view, was the course I was asked to give on social analysis for pastoral theology. My courses at the institute benefited from a regular contact with a large Nairobi slum parish, where I was involved with youth groups and with the catechumenate.

In 1988 I came to the Missionary Institute London and was again directly involved in missionary formation. My students were young men and women preparing to become full-time missionaries. Many had already experienced a short period of pastoral work in a mission context. Besides an introductory course on socio-cultural anthropology, I was expected to teach a course entitled 'Interpretation of Cultures'. The introductory course was straightforward, but it included class presentations by the students which demonstrated their capacity to make a structural analysis.

In the more advanced course, rather than make a list of structuralist and post-structuralist interpretations of culture, I decided to give a practical course on anthropological research for missionaries.

At Gaba, I had given a series of optional evening lectures on fieldwork methods. These I had expanded at Kipalapala to include the methodology of academic study and writing, and much the same course was given at the Nairobi institute. At Kipalapala, to celebrate my return to Tanzania, I wrote a descriptive account of my own Tanzanian fieldwork of ten years earlier.[36] Now, in London, the course I gave was virtually a handbook on the objectives, methods and expectations of anthropological fieldwork. I also participated in the imaginative Maryknoll Institute of African Studies, held each year in Nairobi, Kenya. This is an immersion programme for missionaries and others, in which lectures are combined with guided and supervised field research in and around Nairobi city. My contributions to this programme owed much to my earlier urban research project and to a study, also finished in Nairobi, of health and healing in Africa.[37]

All of this experience in missionary formation convinces me that missionaries require a highly professional and specialized training, particularly in social and cultural anthropology. This must also be combined with an immersion experience, a real research contact with a mission context, which can be integrated with their studies. Above all, missionaries need to learn how to observe and interpret other cultures together with the people of those cultures, and to stimulate them to study and develop them in their turn.

Pre-evangelization and primary evangelization

Redemptoris Missio was written to remind Catholics of their duty to evangelize the growing non-Christian majority of the world's population. The fact that the Church has been implanted in virtually every country of the world can blind us to the existence of unevangelized peoples, but we still have a 'supreme duty to proclaim Christ to all nations'.[38] Evangelizing those who have not yet heard the Good News of the Kingdom is called 'primary evangelization'. 'Pre-evangelization' is the term used for the preparatory phase, during which research is carried out, languages learned, contacts made and the ground prepared for primary evangelization. In fact, it is a necessary step in primary evangelization and is inseparable from it. It is useless to imagine a kind of neutral contact period in which no mutual influence is experienced between the prospective evangelizer and the unevangelized. As soon as the evangelizer appears among them, evangelization has begun.

It is obvious that, as long as Church implantation has not taken place, we are in a situation of primary evangelization. It may not be so evident that primary evangelization should still be a priority after the Church has been founded. The pastoral care of baptized Christians and the fulfilling of the Church's vocation of service to the wider community are, without doubt, grave obligations, but primary evangelization is a vital part of this service. As long as there are populations and communities unreached by the Gospel, the Church has a duty to address them and enter into dialogue with them. The local Church has, therefore, to establish its pastoral priorities, and primary evangelization must be among its first concerns.

There is a confusion, nourished – it must be admitted – by the tenor of the missionary encyclical, between missionary evangelization and primary evangelization. The two are not identical. The former concept is larger and more all-embracing than the latter. It is true, however, that missionaries are oriented towards primary evangelization by their vocation and training for crossing borders. Nowadays, however, being a missionary usually means placing oneself at the service of a foreign local Church. In the aftermath of the Second Vatican Council and of political decolonization, it was sometimes felt that ecclesial maturity meant dispensing with foreign missionaries, and there was much talk of a 'missionary moratorium' and of the 'phasing out' of missionaries. It is obvious that the massive presence of foreign missionaries can impede ecclesial maturity, as does a local Church's reliance on financial and other material resources from abroad. However, the need for foreign missionaries is dictated by many factors, not least by the growing trend of migration and multiculturalism, as well as by new missionary realities such as urbanization. So far from phasing themselves out, missionaries are called to phase themselves into the local Church.

Phasing into a foreign local Church is often difficult and stressful. Missionaries are strangers, and they are not responsible for policy-making. They are obliged to implement policies with which they are not in sympathy, and to follow methods which they find alien. However, if they are really integrated in the local Church of their adoption, they should not be treated simply as workhorses by the local Christian community and its leadership, nor should their opinions be disregarded. They are to be treated as rational collaborators, who have a creative contribution to make. They should even be regarded as enjoying a prophetical role. It frequently happens that missionaries can say and do things that the indigenous clergy and laity cannot. They occupy a liminal or marginal position in the local Church, and they are also channels of inter-Church communication.

Above all, the presence of foreign missionaries in a local Church is a reminder of its obligations towards local and global mission, to respond to local missionary challenges and to send missionaries abroad to other local Churches. Among the Churches of the Reformation this mutual missionary obligation is called 'partnership', and it usually takes the form of a twinning of Churches and/or congregations, not unlike the twinning of towns and cities. In the Catholic Church, we speak today of 'a *koinonia* Church', or of 'mutual ministry' in which mission is multidirectional. Twinning takes place up to a point, but is generally discouraged. The strongest links tend to be those between a local Church and the national or international missionary society which founded it. In any case, primary evangelization should be a priority of local mission, as discerned by the local Church.

Primary evangelization follows the path of interreligious dialogue. It seeks to discover what is of God in the cultural and religious traditions of the unevangelized. It looks for signs of the activity of the Spirit and for the elements of Christian truth which St Justin Martyr called 'seeds of the Word'. It notes the various ways in which the people of these traditions yearn consciously or unconsciously for Christian fulfilment, and it calls them to repentance and conversion. At the appropriate moment, it identifies and names the hitherto unknown Christ, whose Spirit has been at work among them. It speaks to the human imagination about Christ and invites the people to learn about him and consciously to commit themselves in love and freedom to him.

As soon as possible, those who feel drawn by God to adhere to Christ in faith are to be formed into a catechumenal community, and schooled in Christian worship and morality. They should be encouraged to make their own Christian synthesis of faith and culture, and their own applications of the Word to their life and work contexts. Eventually, missionaries should stimulate those who are gifted to give expression to their new faith in terms of their traditional language and culture. With baptism comes the need to maintain viable communities, which can eventually become selfministering, and missionary in their turn, within the world communion of the Catholic Church.

When the primary evangelization phase is complete, the new Christian community still needs nurturing, while it consolidates itself socially and culturally. It may even need a 'second wind' of primary evangelization, a boost – as it were – to keep it on course, even after it has developed ecclesial institutions.

Secularism and the new evangelization

Mention has already been made several times of the so-called 'new evangelization'. Although what is envisaged is technically a second evangelization, it is evidently comparable, if not identical, to primary evangelization. This is especially clear in the case of the secularized, post-Christian Western world. In this situation we are dealing with a majority of people who have no Christian faith. In a recent opinion poll it was discovered that only one-third of the population of Britain had any idea of the Christian meaning of Easter. It is obvious that most of the people questioned have never been effectively confronted by the Good News about Jesus Christ and his Kingdom, and that many of them are not interested, if not negatively disposed towards religion in general.

These people belong to post-Christian countries, that is to say, countries which once possessed a living Christian culture. While this tradition may still be alive for a minority of believing and practising Christians, it is a closed book for the majority. The encyclical *Redemptoris Missio*, however, makes the following controversial statement:

> ... it seems wrong to make no distinction between a people that has never known Christ and a people that has known him and rejected him, but continues to live in a culture permeated to a large extent by Gospel principles. As far as the Faith is concerned these two situations are quite different.[39]

One may ask: In what does the difference consist? People who have never known Christ possess a culture in which the Holy Spirit is at work, and which contains elements of Christian truth, which we call 'seeds of the Word'. There can be no doubt that people of goodwill are influenced by this activity of the Spirit and by these seeds of divine truth, so that they are disposed to respond favourably to evangelization and to find expression for the Gospel in their culture. On the other hand, there may also be people who resist such influences and who reject the message of Christ when it is rendered explicit to them. In the case of people who once possessed a living Christian culture but who now reject Christ, it must be asked why they reject him, and what possible influence their apparently irrelevant culture exercises upon them.

If a majority of people in a secular post-Christian society rejects or ignores Christ, can it be seriously maintained that they are living in a culture in which Gospel principles are at work? Culture is part of the human phenomenon. It does not have some kind of impersonal existence of its own. On the contrary, it is the system of ideas and meanings (expressed in images and norms) by which people relate cognitively, affectively and behaviourally to the world in which they live. If it is suggested that these people who reject or ignore Christ are unconsciously relating to the world in a Christian way, and are somehow Christians in spite of themselves, then such an assertion requires proof. It seems to me that the evidence is to the contrary, and that people in a post-Christian society have suffered a far-reaching cultural impoverishment. All the signs are that they are operating with a modern technological culture which is not only unchristian, but is fundamentally subversive of Gospel principles.

Addressing Christ's message to this type of society is tantamount to a primary evangelization. The Holy Spirit, however, is at work here, as everywhere else in the world. Elements of Christian truth can also be discerned in the modern culture. Some of these might even be traced back to an age when the Christian culture was a living force, or are lodged in the memory of individuals who have a nostalgia for the past. If so, this may provide a starting-point for catechesis.

However, the great problem of post-Christian secularism is the barrier of indifference which separates modern post-Christians from their Christian past, and the privatization and relativization of religion. This barrier has been created by a technological culture which fosters an overriding desire for the material products of technology and the security which they are deemed to provide. The evangelizer is faced with a problem which has never before been encountered on this scale: how to counteract the dehumanizing and dechristianizing effects of technology. Gospel values are basically human values, and people in a secular culture need to be helped to rediscover these values before they can become receptive to the Good News.

As we show in the following chapter, Western technocratic culture is a threat to Christianity all over the world. It is also a grave obstacle to evangelization and to the development of a culturally diversified world Church. Yet a thoroughgoing evangelization demands that the Church be committed to such diversity in unity.

References

1 J. S. La Fontaine, *Initiation: Ritual Drama and Secret Knowledge Across the World* (Harmondsworth: Penguin Books, 1985), gives the general reader a good idea of African initiation.
2 Cf. Clifford Geertz, 'Religion as a Cultural System' in M. Banton (ed.), *Anthropological Approaches to the Study of Religion* (London: Tavistock Publications, 1966), pp. 1–46.
3 *Gaudium et Spes*, 47–52.
4 *Lumen Gentium*, 11.
5 *Evangelii Nuntiandi*, 71.
6 Ibid., 58.
7 *Christifideles Laici*, 30.
8 Cf. Leonardo Boff, *Ecclesiogenesis: Base Communities Reinvent the Church* (London: Collins Liturgical Publications, 1986).
9 *Gaudium et Spes*, 4.
10 *Evangelii Nuntiandi*, 70.
11 *Christifideles Laici*, 23.
12 Canon 230, para. 3.
13 Cf. *Evangelii Nuntiandi*, 70.
14 Cf. Gerald Arbuckle, *Earthing the Gospel* (London: Geoffrey Chapman/ Maryknoll, NY: Orbis Books, 1990).
15 Ibid., pp. 208–20.
16 Ibid., p. 209.
17 Cf. 'Statement from the Gathering of Mission Training Personnel' (Stavanger, 1993; typescript).
18 *Gaudium et Spes*, 54.
19 Thomas S. Kuhn, *The Structure of Scientific Revolutions* (London. University of Chicago Press, 1970), p. 43.
20 Kuhn, op. cit., p. 208; David Bosch, *Transforming Mission – Paradigm Shifts in Theology of Mission* (Maryknoll, NY: Orbis Books, 1991), esp. pp. 183–9.
21 *Redemptoris Missio*, 23.
22 *Evangelii Nuntiandi*, 62–64.
23 *Redemptoris Missio*, 61–76.
24 Ibid., 2, 27, 34, 62–64, 85.
25 Ibid., 32, 33, 49.
26 Ibid., 34, 37, 48.
27 Ibid., 37, 40, 58.
28 Ibid., 4–6, 10.
29 Ibid., 6, 10, 18, 56.
30 Ibid., 52–54.
31 Ibid., 50. There are a few other passing references.
32 Ibid., 65, 90.

33 An early version of the lecture course was published as Aylward Shorter, *African Culture and the Christian Church* (London: Geoffrey Chapman, 1973/ Maryknoll, NY: Orbis Books, 1974).

34 Cf. Aylward Shorter, *African Christian Theology – Adaptation or Incarnation?* (London: Geoffrey Chapman/Maryknoll, NY: Orbis Books, 1975).

35 Later the Catholic University of Eastern Africa.

36 Aylward Shorter, *Priest in the Village: Experiences of African Community* (London: Geoffrey Chapman, 1979).

37 Cf. Aylward Shorter, *The Church in the African City* (London: Geoffrey Chapman/Maryknoll, NY: Orbis Books, 1991); Aylward Shorter, *Jesus and the Witchdoctor – An Approach to Healing and Wholeness* (London: Geoffrey Chapman/Maryknoll, NY: Orbis Books, 1985).

38 *Redemptoris Missio*, 3.

39 Ibid., 37.

4   Obstacles to evangelization

Unity or uniformity?

If faith is to be genuine – fully lived out – it must, in the words of Pope John Paul II, 'become culture'.[1] There is, however, a plurality of cultures. Ergo, the faith must become a plurality of cultures. The logic of this argument is inescapable, and it was perceived by the Second Vatican Council, which taught that the primary reality of the Church is local. The world can only be evangelized by addressing its lived cultural plurality. Only by identifying with this plurality can the Church become a world Church, instead of a culturally imperial Church. These principles have been officially acknowledged, but, as Walbert Buhlmann commented in 1989, there is a snag.

> For all the emphasis on all of this in theory, it is simply
> not permitted in practice. The moment bishops or bishops'
> conferences begin to take concrete steps in the direction of
> actually becoming a local or regional Church, the voice
> of Rome is suddenly heard loud and clear: Halt, in the
> name of unity! *Non licet tibi!* Rome still confuses unity
> with uniformity. And so, instead of becoming the motive
> and model of a legitimate pluriformity, the principle of a
> world Church suddenly becomes a brake: one may do only
> what is already done on the level of the world Church!
> But that cancels all of these beautiful principles. It cancels
> them in practice.[2]

On two separate occasions, and at the request of two different bishops' conferences in Africa, I was personally involved in creating new Eucharistic texts in the Swahili language.[3] Neither of these projects ever saw the light of day, because both were blocked from above. This experience has been repeated in countless places. Before he died two years ago, an African archbishop wrote to me of his great desire for inculturation and of his loneliness in the episcopate where this subject was concerned. He begged for my prayers.[4]

The most serious obstacles to evangelization/inculturation do not come from outside the Church. On the contrary, they arise from within. This is the sombre theme of the present chapter. The most serious obstacles to evangelization are a heritage from an imperial past, from a reluctance to abandon an outmoded paradigm of mission. Does Rome understand the difference between unity and uniformity? Even Pope Paul VI missed the point at first. In his closing speech at the 1974 Synod of Bishops, he declared: 'The content of the faith is either Catholic or it is not'.[5] However, by the time he published *Evangelii Nuntiandi* in the following year, it was clear that he understood the distinction. Since that time, evidence abounds that this understanding is shared in Roman circles. It is not so clear that those who wield power are capable of abandoning their yearning for uniformity in practice.

The success or failure of evangelization in the modern world depends on their doing so. The relentless pursuit of uniformity is alienating the non-Western world. In other words, its consequences are the exact opposite of what is intended; for the attempt to impose a Western model on the world is compromising the world communion of the Catholic Church, as nothing else can.

Mission and cultural interaction

As we approach the third millennium of the Christian era, we can appreciate the historical fact that Catholic Christianity, in the form of one or another Euro-American subculture, has communicated with a multiplicity of non-Western cultures in every part of the world. Such an intercultural process is the factual basis of missionary evangelization and it inevitably influences the dialogue between Gospel and cultures. Acculturation, or the mutual influencing of cultures, is a fact of historical experience, and, in the history of the Church, it has provided the necessary scope for Christian mission. Every culture, whether it communicates or receives the Gospel in the mission process, is called to the conversion we term inculturation.

The colonial episode engenders understandable pessimism about cultural interaction, especially when cultures are discussed in intellectualist or notional terms, rather than in the terms of symbol and experience that we employ in anthropological definitions. Cultures may then appear as Ludwig Wittgenstein's mutually exclusive language-games, with only the possibility of displacing one another, rather than any hope of meaningful interaction.[6] Wittgenstein traced the roots of language to actual experience, and argued that other languages could only be understood with reference to their respective experiences. This led him into an extreme of relativism. Thierry G. Verhelst is among those authors for whom acculturation connotes cultural domination. In spite of this, he believes in the capacity of a culture to reinterpret alien cultural influences creatively.[7] Partly, perhaps, because he adopts Verhelst's pejorative use of the term acculturation, Joseph Donders has attributed to me the suggestion that the subject-matter of inculturation is the 'Western approach to the message of Jesus Christ'.[8] This is a view held by some people in the Church, though not by me.[9] The subject-matter of inculturation is the truth about Jesus Christ, not the culture of the missionaries who make him known. On the other hand, without culture this truth cannot be known to the evangelizers, and without the vehicle of cultural interaction it cannot be made known by them to the evangelized. Whether we like it or not, evangelization supposes an acculturation phase, which hopefully does not obviate eventual creative reinterpretation.[10]

Inculturation and ecclesial communion

As we have already noted in Chapter 2, there is no model of successful inculturation on offer to the world. All cultures, even – perhaps especially – the Euro-American, are ripe for evangelization and conversion, but this does not alter the fact that Jesus Christ confronts cultures through a creative cultural reinterpretation, triggered by the intercultural process. Moreover, if mission itself takes place at the intercultural level, it is equally true that the visible structures of ecclesial communion operate at that same level.

Many people have been genuinely inspired by Vincent Donovan's rediscovery of Christianity among the Maasai of East Africa.[11] His book continues to impart a compelling freshness to the idea of mission. According to Donovan, however, a missionary has only to present God and Jesus Christ and his work is finished. The rest he can safely leave to the people he has evangelized: the invention of the liturgy, the shape of the local Church, the form of its ministry; because their insights and models, though different from those of Euro-American culture, have true and lasting validity.[12] While it is true that local Churches throughout the world should not become carbon copies of Churches in Europe or America, it must be stressed that there is no culturally neutral

Gospel, no culture-free knowledge of Jesus Christ. Moreover, if it is to survive, the Maasai Church cannot exist in a vacuum.[13] It has to relate to other inculturated forms of Christianity in a fellowship of interdependent Churches. Ecclesial maturity does not consist in self-encapsulation, but in the capacity to give, receive and mutually invigorate within a *koinonia*. Donovan demonstrates that the Maasai must break free from their parochialism, if they are to become Christians, but he does not consider their place in a Catholic communion that is visibly and hierarchically structured, and which guarantees a bond of faith, sacrament and ministry among all the local Churches.[14]

In discussing the cultural implications of ecclesial communion in the Catholic Church it is necessary to affirm at the outset that it is visibly and concretely structured. While it is true that the concept of inculturation favours an ecclesiology of communion, it cannot dispense with the other basic ecclesiological component, that of hierarchy. Catholic communion rests on the premise of a teaching authority exercised in matters of faith, sacrament and ministry, and this authority includes a Petrine ministry with, at its present stage of historical development, an immediate, worldwide jurisdiction. Catholic communion does not resemble the Anglican concept of a family of autonomous Churches, threatened with becoming, in Archbishop Robert Runcie's words, an 'impaired communion', or at worst, in the words of the Eames Commission, a form of 'institutionalized schism'.[15] Even Anglicans are now faced with the need to reinforce the structures that hold them together, and the 1988 Lambeth Conference accordingly decided to strengthen the meeting of the 27 Primates, and called for Inter-Anglican Doctrinal and Liturgical Commissions.[16] Since then, we have observed the acute problems of internal communion in the Church of England, after the General Synod's controversial vote in 1992 for the priestly ordination of women.

What is at issue in this discussion is not the reality of (Roman) Catholic communion, but its contingent form and functions. Either this communion is used to block inculturation, or it is used to promote it. It can uphold either cultural monocentrism (uniformity) or cultural polycentrism (unity in diversity, pluriformity). As we have seen, there are no convincing signs that authority is encouraging the praxis of diversification and pluriformity in the Church at large. Rather the reverse. Indeed an Anglican observer, Paul Avis, has remarked that, after the demise of the Eastern totalitarian regimes, 'the only relic of centralized authoritarianism in Europe will be the Vatican'.[17] Be that as it may, it is clear that a culturally polycentric Catholic Church remains, for the present, a dream. It is not, however, an impossible dream.

On the contrary, it is the strictly logical consequence of an honest acceptance of the inculturation concept, which, in turn, is an inherent requirement of evangelization and true Catholicity. Historically, it is the inevitable outcome of missionary expansion in the nineteenth and twentieth centuries.

The requirements of a culturally polycentric Church

By definition, inculturation cannot be imposed from the centre, but it can be obstructed by it. There are those who feel that the obstruction of creative pluriformity in the local Churches contributes to a loss of credibility, perhaps even to the marginalization of authority in the Church. Pedro Arrupe, Superior General of the Society of Jesus, went so far as to speak of a possible 'crisis of unity' when he spoke at the 1977 Synod of Bishops. He listed four difficulties in realizing inculturation.

> The first is an instinctive fear when confronted by new ideas and the people who present them.
> Secondly, pluralism is thought to be a danger for the Church when in fact the crisis of unity often results from an insufficient pluralism that makes it difficult for some to express and live their faith within their own culture.
> Thirdly, a flight from reality – due to fear of unavoidable dangers we can be led to separate faith from real life.
> Fourthly, the lack of a fair and sober assessment of modern culture, however materialistic, irreligious and atheistic it may seem, can result in the teaching and practice of a faith that is conceptual, divorced from culture, not incarnated.[18]

The progress report on *Sects or New Religious Movements*, published in 1985 by four Vatican secretariats, recognizes the truth of Arrupe's words. The need for inculturation was one of the lessons to be learned from the sects.

> The question of inculturation is a fundamental one. It is particularly stressed by the responses from Africa which reveal a feeling of estrangement to western forms of worship and ministry which are often quite irrelevant to people's cultural environment and life situation. One respondent declared: 'Africans want to be Christians. We have given them accommodation, but no home ... They want a simpler Christianity, integrated into all aspects of daily life, into the sufferings, joys, work, aspirations, fears and needs of

the African ... The young recognize in the Independent
Churches a genuine vein of the African tradition of doing
things religious.'[19]

This verdict is reinforced by an eloquent passage in the *Instrumentum Laboris* of the 1994 African Synod:

Those responsible in pastoral matters should analyse the
nature of inculturation of Christianity in Africa and its
capacity to constitute vibrant ecclesial communities, the role
of the laity, the response to the thirst for spiritual
experience and the Word of God, as well as the reply to be
given to the vital questions posed by suffering, sickness
and death.[20]

Even if secessions can be forestalled, there is also the danger of
a 'self-help Church' in which outward conformity conceals a far-reaching internal heterodoxy and syncretism, somewhat along the
lines of the African religions of Brazil, with their Portuguese
Catholic veneer.[21] It is becoming clear that inculturation will not
wait. As we shall see later on in this chapter, there are other
reasons connected with what Arrupe called 'modern culture' – and
especially urbanization and communications technology – which
make the praxis of inculturation an urgent matter. 'The Latin
Church', wrote J.-Y. Calvez, 'must renounce its superiority complex and monopoly of forms of expression.'[22]

What, then, are the characteristics and requirements of a culturally polycentric Catholic Church? A good starting-point is the
lament of the Zaïrean theologian, Oscar Bimwenyi, already summarized in Chapter 2. Here are his own uncompromising words
about the Christian life of Africans:

They pray to God with a liturgy that is not theirs. They
live according to a pre-existing morality which is not the
conversion of their own previous morality under the action
of God's grace and the breath of the Holy Spirit. They
are ruled by a Canon Law which is not a law born from
the conversion to Christ of social and juridical realities
inherent in the universe to which they belong ... They
reflect – when indeed they reflect – using philosophical
and theological systems secreted by the meditation and
reflection of the other Christian communities which
evangelized them.[23]

Bimwenyi's sober assessment offers an agenda for 'earthing', 'rooting', 'grounding' or 'inserting' the Gospel in a local culture.[24]
Such metaphors echo Paul VI's concern that the Gospel should be

transposed into cultural or anthropological language, and not merely into a semantic or literary one.[25] It is useless to proclaim the Gospel, if it is not allowed to take root. Christianity's growth depends on this, and this condition, in turn, implies the abandonment of monocultural uniformity. A theologian from India bluntly declares:

> Christianity, with its universal message, cannot grow as a religion today, unless it abandons its preference for western culture, with its rational, technically minded, masculine bias, and opens up to the feminine, intuitive understanding of reality in the east.[26]

Eurocentrism versus polycentrism

The eighteenth-century 'Enlightenment' and its aftermath strengthened the misguided conviction of European Catholics that they were in possession of absolute cultural norms, but although lip-service is now paid to cultural pluralism, Euro-American Catholicism has not wholly shed its culture blindness.[27] This is shown by a conscious or unconscious process of theological obfuscation in much official writing about inculturation.

Historically, Christian evangelization has enjoyed its greatest apparent successes wherever there was a technological culture-differential between evangelizer and evangelized. This explains, for example, why the Church today is stronger in Latin America and Africa than in Asia. The success, however, has been achieved at the price of cultural domination. This culture-differential also underlies the contemporary consciousness of a 'global village' or 'one world'. Euro-American technocratic culture is a totalitarian world process that has created a global monetary system, provoked a worldwide industrial revolution, internationalized productive capital and – for good or ill (mostly ill) – influenced global ecology.[28] At the global or macro-level, cultural diversity is disappearing under the influence of this process of modernization, the chief instrument of which is urbanization.[29] By the end of the twentieth century half the world's population will be urban-dwelling. Besides creating ecological problems, modernization/urbanization is a force for secularization, for cultural disorientation at the micro-level and for increasing the disparities between rich and poor.[30] It is not surprising that inculturation assumes considerable importance in ex-colonial countries where the recovery or redefinition of traditional culture is jeopardized by this world process.[31] At the macro-level of technology there is no exotic alternative to Euro-

American modernization. There is no option but to assume the whole package. While it threatens to wipe out local, cultural traditions, the world system itself fails to meet the basic needs of humanity, and, indeed, has no real substance as a cultural system.[32] On the contrary, it appears to undermine human sensibilities and render human beings less compassionate.[33] It is, as it were, a worldwide movement of 'anti-culture'.[34]

If this viewpoint is accepted, it is difficult not to agree with Johan Baptist Metz that 'the secular Europeanization of the world is not an innocent vehicle' for the universal propagation of the Church's message.[35] The alternatives are spelt out by Rottlander: either the Church concludes that inculturation is a piece of hopeless romanticism and jumps on the Euro-American capitalist bandwagon, or it accepts inculturation and makes a credible bid for a polycultural Christianity.[36] The first alternative implies the subversion of the Gospel itself; the second, in the words of Michael Amaladoss, 'is a call to uphold human and religious values as the basis and inspiration of culture in a secular and technological world' – a world which separates religion and culture as a matter of course.[37] This is not a question of expediency, but one which belongs to the Church's own vocation to meet 'others in their otherness'.[38] Non-Western cultures are resisting the logic of Euro-American secular domination, and it belongs to the Church to side with those who feel threatened, not to assist in the destructive process itself by drawing peoples into the secularizing vortex. It may even be that Euro-America needs to draw on the spiritual resources of the non-Western world to fight its own battle with the secularizing and dehumanizing process, a battle in which we must not despair of victory, as Pedro Arrupe pointed out at the 1977 Synod of Bishops.[39] Gerald Arbuckle in the Philippines, for example, has recently applied the fruit of his non-Western experience to the inculturation problems of Euro-America, Australia and New Zealand.[40]

Eurocentrism in official inculturation theology

Inculturation is now so much a part of theological discourse in the Church that there are few neo-conservatives sufficiently courageous to contest it explicitly. One of the few is Aidan Kavanagh of Yale University, who acquiesces in the label 'reactionary'.[41] Kavanagh fears that inculturation will lead to the local politicization of the liturgy and the 'dispersal of the Church itself as a worshipping community'.[42] He writes:

Our First World will necessarily influence the other Worlds of the planet, even decreasingly, because our World is the one farthest ahead in power in all its aspects – intellectual, economic, military, educational, and so on. Our World's inevitable cultural power, even in decline, is necessarily far greater now than anything the British brought to bear on their colonies in the nineteenth and early twentieth century.[43]

It is rare to find such complacency in the face of Euro-American secularizing world culture. Kavanagh sees the answer as loyalty to the Gospel in the cultural forms of the evangelizer, and, although he tries to disarm in advance the critics who would accuse him of advocating a *laissez-faire* policy, he appears to believe that inculturation is a mystery that will develop organically by itself.

Another well-known exponent of Western monoculturalism is Cardinal Josef Ratzinger, who puts his faith in the worldwide spread of European thought and in 'the universal significance of Christian thought as it has evolved in the West'.[44] Recently, he urged the bishops of Asia to give up the term 'inculturation' and replace it with the word 'interculturality'.[45] The cardinal pointed out quite correctly that missionary evangelization takes place through a meeting of cultures, but he ruled out the possibility of one culture dominating the other. He went on to imply that the Christian faith is communicated through Western culture and to say that this culture is 'fused' with the evangelized culture. His dislike of the term 'inculturation' is apparently based on his opposition to an authentic re-expression of the faith in terms of the evangelized culture. His approach is close to that of Pius XII and the pre-conciliar Church, which favoured the idea of a monolithic hybrid Christian culture, in which the cultural matrix was Western.[46] That so eminent and influential a personality in the Church should identify Christian universality with Western cultural forms is disturbing, to say the least, but it provides a clue to Roman curial policy.

Generally, however, those who oppose cultural polycentrism in the Church take refuge in abstract and minimalist versions of inculturation theory, while upholding Eurocentrism in practice. Gregory Baum notes the curious contradiction between official affirmations concerning inculturation and the participatory society, on the one hand, and the *magisterium*'s return to centralization and authoritarianism, on the other. As in other areas of doctrinal and moral teaching, the Church's failure to follow its own pronouncements fatally weakens the power of its message.[47]

To take abstractionism first, a major form consists in assuming that the Church, Gospel or faith pre-exists, and accompanies, the act of evangelization in a culturally disembodied form.[48] The idea seems to be that there is an 'essence of the Gospel',[49] that there are 'core values' or an 'invariant core',[50] that culture is an extrinsic, separable phenomenon, a 'husk' enclosing a 'kernel', 'soil' receiving a 'seed', a 'form' requiring 'content', or accidents in relation to substance in Thomistic philosophy.[51] In fact, as we have seen, religion is by definition a cultural system and is integrally linked to culture.[52] This is equally true of the Christian Gospel, the supracultural validity of which consists in its capacity for cultural re-expression in a series of historical inculturations stretching back in a trajectory of meaning to the events and outlooks of the New Testament, and appealing to authentic values in every human, cultural tradition.[53] We do not live in a world of essences, nor do magisterial faith statements arise in some privileged supracultural sphere; rather the Gospel travels throughout history from one inculturated form to another.[54]

Minimalization consists in playing down inculturation as a two-way process. In Roman documents considerable emphasis is placed on the Church or Gospel which 'penetrates', 'transforms', 'heals', 'elevates', 'enriches', or 're-centres' cultures.[55] Cultures are said to be 'introduced into the life of the Church'.[56] *L'Osservatore Romano* even went so far as to entitle an address of Pope John Paul II in 1983: 'The Church Creator of Culture in Her Relation with the Whole World'.[57] The Church is thus envisaged as a cultural entity, standing over against all other cultures. Little or nothing is said of inculturation leading to a new creation, or bearing new fruit for the Church; of cultures discovering, interpreting, realizing or re-expressing the Gospel; of new insights that can enrich the universal communion of particular Churches.[58] N. Standaert has even noticed that a quotation, in a papal address, from *Evangelii Nuntiandi* edited out the reference to the cultural re-expression of the Gospel and stopped short at the evangelizer's work of transposition.[59]

Another minimalist tactic is to exaggerate the need for slowness in carrying out inculturation, in order to lessen its assumed risks and dangers. Writers such as Adrian Hastings and Gerald Arbuckle point out that sound inculturation does not suddenly happen, but is encouraged to grow, depending, as it does, on a personal and cultural conversion.[60] Others, however, call for patience because they do not believe in the need for any effective intervention to bring it about.[61] Against this, other writers – especially from Africa – speak of inculturation as requiring vital and urgent action.[62] This is because they feel that the *status quo* is deteriorating; Christians lead a divided life; religious education is superficial; syncretism and secularism are fast gaining the upper hand. Worse still, expectations are being created by official teaching which are not being fulfilled in practice. Inculturation requires urgent practical implementation if there is to be effective evangelization. Without a doubt, minimalism reflects and upholds the actual *status quo* in the Church, according to which centralized authority usurps the culturally pluriform vernacular of faith.

Somewhat surprisingly, the *Lineamenta* of the 1994 African Synod tackles the question of the culturally polycentric Church. It does this almost absent-mindedly when considering the necessity of communication among the different particular Churches.

> In fact, lack of communication could destroy the unity existent among the diverse forms of inculturation which can bear fruit *only when communication is reciprocal and enduring*. True inculturation provides richness for all the Particular Churches and for the Universal Church, because *it is a question of deepening the faith*. However, until this is able to be realized, each Church *should constantly speak a language common to all* and remain open to fraternal correction.[63]

This passage affirms that inculturation can only bear fruit in a situation of enduring ecclesial reciprocity. No one form of inculturation is to be imposed on all the particular Churches. Rather, the universal Church should consist in diverse forms of inculturation which communicate with one another, and deepen the faith for each. This is exactly the model of a diversified, polycentric Church, engaging in cross-cultural exchange and communication. Unfortunately, in spite of all this, the paragraph takes away with one hand what it gives with the other. It appears to advocate the postponement of this new vision of Church. It is not yet 'able to be realized'. For the time being the particular Churches 'must constantly speak a language common to all and remain open to fraternal correction'. This looks very much as if the local Churches are not to be given any practical autonomy for the foreseeable future, must operate with structures of communion biased in favour of Euro-American culture, and must accept surveillance from outside. If these words mean what they say, then they are nothing less than a call for a moratorium on inculturation itself.

That the African Synod's *Lineamenta* can so clearly define the ideal, and in the same breath toss it on one side, is profoundly shocking. One should, perhaps, be grateful that the ideal is recognized at all, and that the blatant discrepancy between theory and practice is so openly paraded for all to see. Yet one can only hope that the African Synod will rise up against this expediency and denounce any cynical postponement of inculturation praxis. 'Deepening the faith' and a 'language common to all' are phrases which stand in flagrant contradiction to one another. Inculturation comes about through experimentation and praxis, not through uncommitted speculation.

The dynamic of inculturation praxis

Who or what is inculturated? Certain possibilities have already been ruled out. The subject of inculturation is not the Gospel, in the sense of a core or essence rationally paraphrased into propositional form. As Metz points out, the dogmas and faith-statements of the past require decoding, if we are to understand them today, because they belong to alien inculturations.[64] The Gospel is not a theological treatise, but a history, at the centre of which is the God-man, born in Bethlehem and 'raised up' in Jerusalem.[65] What is inculturated is a trajectory or path of meaning which goes back through the events of Church history to those of the New Testament. The person of Jesus Christ is made imaginatively credible to people of the evangelized culture, through missionary evangelization. Through grace, the evangelized are enabled to respond to Christ's self-gift, and to inform and construct their lives in accordance with the 'Christic model'.[66]

The fact that the Gospel is basically a history of events which carry a coherent meaning, going back to Christ in the New Testament, entails two further consequences. One is that the cultures of the Bible are necessarily privileged and respected as the *ne plus ultra* in cultural decoding.[67] The second is, as we saw in Chapter 2, that a historic Church accumulates a currency or patrimony of cultural elements, either contingent or necessary, which is communicated through acculturation and which survives in great part as a syncretic component in Christianity's inculturated forms.[68] There is still a dangerous tendency in official Church documents to imply that this patrimony is a culture, and even to equate it with a universally significant Euro-American culture. This patrimony includes the residue of previous inculturations, as well as the outcome of mutual invigoration and enrichment in the contemporary communion of Churches.[69] It is a multicultural phenomenon which assists the Church in passing 'from one kind of clarity to another' in its developing understanding of the faith.[70] It is a naive oversimplification to identify this patrimony with the culture of Europe, even if that culture is seen to be what it is in reality, a complex phenomenon of astonishing diversity.

Inculturation as diversification

J.-Y. Calvez has written: 'Inculturation is diversification', and other theologians have spoken of a 'polycentric Christianity' with a diversity of cultural roots.[71] Who are then the agents of a polycentric inculturation? The obvious response is that they are the regional particular Churches. Even Aidan Kavanagh wants inculturation left to practising, baptized Christians, rather than to hierarchs, commissions, theologians or even pastors.[72] This liberality, however, is somewhat negated by his insistence on rigid control by episcopal conferences and Roman curial congregations. We come back, therefore, to the question of ecclesiology. In the documents of the Second Vatican Council an ecclesiology of communion emerges from the background of an older, pyramidic universalism. Angel Anton has argued convincingly for the collegiality of episcopal conferences, provinces and patriarchates, in spite of recent attempts to deny their theological significance.[73] *De facto*, episcopal conferences are being given more and more responsibilities and they constitute in reality a form of communion among the particular Churches or dioceses. The episcopal function is by its very nature collegial and episcopal ordination is a collegial act, carried out by a neighbouring bishop or bishops.[74] Collegial responsibility and collegial action belong, therefore, to the episcopal function. The praxis of inculturation is a genuine development of the theology of the local Church.[75]

By definition, the *analogum princeps* of the local or particular Church is the diocese, but it is clear that a diocese can seldom be identified with the culture, cluster of cultures, or context that is the object of inculturation.[76] Although the diocese is, in reality, a flexible unit, being large or small in extent, densely or sparsely populated, as the case may be, ethnic cultures frequently overlap diocesan boundaries and even those of national episcopal conferences. There are also unstructured, culturally similar or identical, groups of nomads and migrants present in dioceses which are not even geographically contiguous.[77] For these reasons, bilateral, regional, and even continental relationships among episcopal conferences may be of greater cultural or contextual significance than relations among individual dioceses.[78]

The joint initiatives of dioceses and episcopates are at present firmly controlled by the Holy See, under the provisions of the 1983 Code of Canon Law. According to Legrain, the code's Catholicity is open to question and its compromise between centralization and decentralization is poorly formulated.[79] More disturbing, perhaps, is the fact that its understanding of mission is outdated.

It follows the obsolete missionary paradigm. The code sees missionary activity as going from the centre to the periphery, from Euro-America to the South, when – from a missionary point of view – the Church is more than ever before a *koinonia* of local Churches, reaching out to one another in their needs.[80] Ecclesial maturity is measured today by a capacity for interdependence, by the ability both to give from poverty and to receive in humility. Although pastoral sensitivity, diversity of application, conflict with established custom and grants of dispensation ensure a varied exercise, the 1983 Code of Canon Law remains bound to its culture of origin. This can be seen, for example, in the cultural parallelism which results from the implementation of the Church's marriage law, or from the extraordinary attempt – in Canon 1083 – to legislate for the entire world concerning the age of maturity for marriage.[81] If there is one conclusion to be drawn, it is that of the canonist, Piskaty, that the Roman Curia cannot make binding decisions for the local Church.[82] Many, if not most, episcopates have yet to be persuaded of this, and their members have often been appointed, in defiance of local preferences, because of this.[83]

If inculturation cannot be conferred upon the local Church by a centralized administration, this authority is nevertheless all too capable of obstructing the process, chiefly by withholding permission for experimentation and approval for local initiatives. Yet, even here, it has been pointed out that the spontaneous initiatives of oral cultures frequently escape the surveillance of the literate bureaucracy which needs texts and documents submitted for approval or disapproval. The early history of the Zaïre Mass is a case in point. This is inculturation from below, the only valid inculturation, and it explains the importance of initiatives taken at the grass roots, particularly in the basic communities.[84] When inculturation becomes a lived and popular reality, it is unstoppable, and official disapproval runs the risk of provoking schisms and secessions, as Pedro Arrupe foresaw.

The impact of communications technology

If evangelization is essentially a process of communication, then it cannot avoid being affected by the modern means of social communication. They are also obviously relevant to the question of inculturation. In fact, it is to a large extent through these media that the Euro-American macroculture is imposed on the indigenous traditions of the non-Western world. The agencies from which world news emanates are situated in the West; the printed periodicals with the biggest world circulations originate there; most of the films shown worldwide are produced in the West; most of the pre-recorded video cassettes obtainable are Western; and now Western satellite television programmes are being beamed all over the world. The impact of Western printed and electronic media on the rest of the world is comprehensive and devastating. The cultural message which is transmitted is one of an increasingly introspective and self-critical – albeit arrogant – Western society, beset with problems of violent crime, drug-taking and sexual permissiveness. It is a culture which imposes new forms of paternalism through its ecological concerns and its liberal ideology.

It is often argued that only the urban populations of the non-Western world are affected. That is not true. No doubt the readers of foreign publications and the viewers of foreign videos and satellite television are primarily members of the urban élite, but consider the following facts also. In many non-Western countries cities and towns are growing twice as fast as national populations. By the end of the first quarter of the next millennium, half the population will be city-dwelling. Because of the reigning urban bias, which is certainly linked to urban technological superiority, such cities and towns exert a disproportionate influence on the surrounding rural areas. They wield the power and they set the trends. Returning migrants carry back to the countryside the values they have learned in the city. The rural-dwelling population may see fewer films and watch fewer videos than the city dwellers, but the impact of audio-visual media of this kind is likely to have a greater effect on the less sophisticated and less literate peasant population.

Rural populations are most influenced by vernacular print media and especially – in an oral society – by radio. Radio broadcasting is the primary means of disseminating news and issuing directives. Although much of the content is misunderstood, and the radio is commonly used to provide a continuous background of sound and music in houses, bars and shops, its influence eventually percolates down to the grass roots. For this reason authoritarian governments exercise an uncompromising control over newspapers and broadcasts. In many non-Western countries national newspapers and broadcasting corporations are owned or censored by government. Single-party regimes use these media for political propaganda. When a military *coup d'état* takes place to overthrow a dictatorial regime, the national radio and television centre is always one of the vital installations to defend or to capture – along with the airport, the barracks and the presidential palace. I remember my first experience of an African *coup d'état*. It was in Uganda, on 25 January 1971. The day after the coup the same newscaster who had formerly praised the fallen president to the skies now publicly vilified him. It was an extraordinary demonstration of how dictatorial regimes use the media.

State monopoly or censorship of the means of communication: television, radio and press, can amount to the denial of a human right. It is an interference in the freedom of communication. As such, it aids and abets alien cultural domination and it promotes subservience to the self-interested policies of a Western-dominated world. The unethical manipulation of the media endorses injustice and suppresses a critical public opinion. The modern means of communication, however, are here to stay. Let us look at the media revolution, and the way in which it is affecting the world.

A few minutes' reflection can tell us that the media are altering our lives and changing our relationships with one another – even with God. This is not a question of crudely blaming the media for a rise in the level of crime, violence and sexual offences in society. The portrayal of such things may also have the cathartic effect of getting them out of the social system. The pastoral instruction *Communio et Progressio* of 1971 was less narrow than the Vatican II decree *Inter Mirifica*, and recognized that it was naive to put all or most of the blame on the media for declining moral standards. However, television, for example, does affect family life and the upbringing of children. When I was a child, in the days before television, my mother would read a book to us in the evening while we drew, painted or played with toys. On other evenings, we gathered around the piano to sing, and every day we recited the rosary together as a family. Such family activity is difficult, if not impossible, to maintain nowadays, in the face of competition from the all-absorbing 'box'.

Nowadays, by the time children go to school for the first time, they have already spent more hours in front of the television set than they will ever spend in a school classroom. At their most impressionable age, children have already received images and experiences which will stay with them for the rest of their lives. They are even too sophisticated for children's television. Parental supervision is next to impossible, yet it is the responsibility of parents to help their children develop a critical discernment of their viewing, and to answer their children's questions on the myriad topics which fill the small screen.

Television and the other modern media transmit to the viewing, listening and reading public a succession of stories, and it is for its story value that every item is judged. There is no form of communication as powerful and persuasive as story-telling, and without stories the Church fails as a communicator. Discussions, monologues, hymn-singing, liturgical services are all eclipsed by the story. Some of the media stories are inspiring and elevating; some are depraving and demoralizing. Whatever their character, the stories appear one after the other in random succession, religious and Christian stories among them.

Television, radio and journalism have many positive aspects. They teach new interests. For example, because of them, classical music, opera and ballet are receiving greater attention in Europe and winning larger audiences. Serious contemporary drama has a platform; and people are more ecologically aware as a result of programmes about animals and the natural environment. The media also help one another. For example, television and radio programmes review books, plays and films or summarize the editorials of daily and weekly newspapers. The relationship between the media and public opinion is instructive. With the extensive, multilateral media coverage of recent wars in the Falkland Islands, the Gulf region, and former Yugoslavia, and in spite of media manipulation by the military and civilian authorities, belligerent governments have had to account more openly for their actions. There is a limit to what the viewing public finds acceptable.

On the other hand, the media are used to create a mythology: the 'surgical' military strike, for example, the 'paranoia' of the Iraqi president, the 'rape' of Kuwait in the Gulf War, the 'culpability' of the Bosnian Serbs in the Yugoslavian civil war. Such mythologies create illusions in the minds of viewers and listeners, which rob people of the capacity to make a genuine moral response to events. The programme producers and the correspondents do not merely reflect the prejudices and assumptions of the viewing, listening and reading public. They do that, of course, but they also have an agenda of their own. This agenda is dictated by commerce and the profit motive – by what can be marketed. The relationship of commercial breaks to ordinary television programmes is far from fortuitous. Moreover, as state-controlled systems give way to satellite and cable channels, as local radio comes more and more into its own and an ever increasing choice is available to the public, commercial factors progressively dominate the media scene. Worldwide television and broadcasting networks are created to market their product. Local editions of newspapers transmitted by satellite do the same. There is even a worldwide television network from Japan, created in order to promote the sale of television sets.

On every side content is sacrificed to process and profit, and a small circle of media people communicate to an ever growing audience. In the new media culture, image counts for more than reality. The trivial is made to seem important and the important trivialized. Television and radio are suffused with self-admiration and self-congratulation. Feedback and criticism are manipulated and neutralized, because the media people are the final arbiters and interpreters of everything that goes out. Those who live under the spell of the media lead vicarious 'shadow lives'. Soap operas and serials provide them with a 'shadow family' and with friends and neighbours to replace the flesh and blood people next door. Conversation is not about real, personal experience, but always about what one has seen on the box. Compulsive 'soap' viewers may even sometimes need psychiatric help to break their addiction.

What has been called 'cassettization' is another consequence of modern media, in particular of the video and tape recorder. All our vicarious experiences can be trapped on a cassette. We can record programmes we might otherwise have missed. We can build up a library of our favourite movies. We may never go to a real-life concert or theatre, but we can enjoy Mozart or Shakespeare on cassette. We not only lead vicarious lives, but 'cassettized' lives as well. 'We had the experience, but missed the meaning', wrote T. S. Eliot. In the cassette culture, we miss the experience as well as the meaning.

Is this too negative a picture? I believe it is an accurate enough image of what is happening in the technological cultures of the Western world. The so-called Third World is far from reaching this stage yet, but it is already dominated by those, at home or abroad, who live in this way. Already world television networks are available, and non-Western countries are beginning to be flooded with video recordings emanating from Europe and America. They are the more vulnerable to this electronic invasion in the measure in which their own technology and media development lag behind those of the West.

A good example of this is provided by the history of African cinema. A recent BBC publication begins:

> African cinema epitomises the basic problems of the Third World: lack of capital to produce; no infrastructure for production and distribution; no export markets; shortage of skilled technicians; and dependence on superficial aid.[85]

In English-speaking Africa, film units were operating in colonial times producing films intended to introduce Africans to European ways. These units ceased production before political independence, and virtually nothing replaced them. The Commonwealth does next to nothing to promote the film industry in Africa. Even the more co-operative French government has had moments of hesitation, as a result of pressure from African governments. It is not surprising that over 80 per cent of international African film makers are French-speaking: famous directors like Idrissa

Ouédraogo of Burkina Faso, Sembéné Ousmane of Senegal and Souleymane Cissé of Mali.

African governments are ambivalent towards African film making. They wish to control this powerful medium, and African film makers choose themes which are too close to reality for their liking. Rather than allow their citizens to see the masterpieces created by their own artists and directors, they prefer to lull African audiences with the illusory escapism provided by Hollywood westerns or James Bond. Western cinema is yet another drug intended to immobilize the population – the bread and circuses of twentieth-century imperialism. It has often happened that African governments have only woken up to the existence of African film making when an African film wins a prize at the Cannes Film Festival. Fortunately, there are now film festivals at Ouagadougou and Carthage, and since the Pan-African Meeting on Social Communications at Ibadan in 1973, the Catholic Church's OCIC offers an African film award.

It is estimated that there are 2,500 cinemas in Africa for a population of 600 million. From the 9,000 or so films screened in Africa each year foreign film companies make a profit 60 times higher than that of African film companies. Even when African governments succeed in controlling the cinema in their countries, this does not help African film makers, although public reaction to African films is very positive. While there are a number of well-known African directors, there are very few technicians. At present there are film schools in Ghana, Burkina Faso, Kenya and Tanzania. Financing for production, however, still comes from Europe and bodies like UNESCO.

The impact of print media

The technology and financing of print media are much more within the bounds of non-Western possibilities. Non-Western print media are better able to compete with foreign publications, although they frequently reproduce syndicated material from abroad, and satellites are beginning to transmit foreign journals for local printing. The main enemies of the print media are the high levels of illiteracy and the curtailment of press freedom by governments. Authoritarian regimes are particularly sensitive to criticism or the publication of opinions which differ from the official view. The list of banned publications and editors in detention is, alas, a long one.

The Second Vatican Council Decree on the means of social

communication *Inter Mirifica* was declared 'unworthy of the Council' by Cardinal Heenan of Great Britain.[86] It was certainly a disappointing document, and in any case it announced its own supersession by a Pontifical Commission which would produce its own pastoral instruction. When this appeared as *Communio et Progressio* in 1971, it was hailed as a much more satisfactory document. Among its more notable recommendations was the plea for better communication within the Church itself. Its theology, however, was weak. The argument it put forward was that the Church must make use of the 'marvellous technical inventions which foster communication', because Christ, its founder, was himself 'the perfect communicator'. In 1983 the secretary general of the World Association for Christian Communications, himself a Catholic priest with communications experience in Africa, made a critique of this hallowed phrase during a meeting in Rome.[87] A communicator, he argued, is only perfect when his audience gets the message. When Jesus was on earth, he was rejected by the leaders of his people and misunderstood by his own followers, right up to the moment when he ascended into heaven. The only apostle who can be said to have understood him was Judas, and he precipitated the crisis, in the hope of deflecting Jesus from his purpose. Perfect communicator or failed communicator? Did not the redemptive power of Jesus reside in what the world considered a failure?

In the first Agnellus Andrew Lecture, delivered in 1990 at Broadcasting House, London, Dr Colin Morris argued that the modern means of communication are a vehicle of power inherently unsuited to the message of a crucified Christ. The massive investment in electronic media by new fundamentalist movements from North America is a display of earthly, not spiritual, power. The lamentable moral example provided by some American televangelists is a commentary on the ability of media power to corrupt. In using the new technology, Christians must not succumb to its powerful tendency to dominate others through illusion and manipulation of response. Their message is the Cross, not the crusade. Whatever means are used, nothing can replace humble conviction and faith translated into the real life activity of love.

When a so-called 'God-slot' is provided in a programme of continuous sound or vision, it must either obey the canons of contemporary communication consumerism, or stick out like a sore thumb as a specialized item for the initiated few. In the first case, it is relativized for the undifferentiated masses. In the second case, it is preaching to the converted. Slipping the Christian message in among the other messages of the secular technological culture put out by state television or radio may be a form of primary evangelization, but the enormous expenditure of resources which would be involved in setting up Church broadcasting systems would not be justified. If evangelization is about communicating the Good News to receptive audiences, then it is better to devote the resources to film, video and audio production. These products can be used in many different catechetical settings, and suitable items can be offered to national and local broadcasting systems.

If secular film production in non-Western countries suffers from lack of financial, technical and human resources, then the Catholic Church in these countries *a fortiori* suffers from the same disadvantages. However, Catholic organizations have been in existence since before the Second Vatican Council: UNDA for radio and television, OCIC for cinema and UCAP for press. Structures have been set up for channelling funds, initiating projects and training communicators, but these structures are seldom as effective as they should be. The Church must hasten to comply with the directives of *Communio et Progressio* and of its own organizations. Efforts must be made to set up production units, so that catechetical and broadcast material can be provided. The new video technology makes this work much easier today. Video camcorders and video cassette recorders are becoming more plentiful, and they are relatively easy to use. The Church should make the best possible use of this versatile medium.

At the same time, an important point made by *Communio et Progressio* should be remembered. People, especially parents, teachers and pastors, must be helped to use the medium constructively in community. People must be taught to evaluate, to criticize, to build on what they see, and not to remain passive consumers only. They must learn to relate the medium to real life. Only in this way can the media begin to be neutralized as an obstacle to evangelization and be converted into its instrument.

Secrecy and censorship in the Church

In spite of the strong recommendations of *Communio et Progressio* for a free, two-way flow of information within the Church itself, and for an openness in communicating with the world, Catholic authorities seem not to have taken this advice wholeheartedly.[88] The Church, and particularly the Pope, frequently receive a bad press. Part of the reason for this is the secrecy with which the Church traditionally operates. Catholic bishops and priests seem not to be at ease in dealing with the press. Even when press offices are set up, they are undermined by leaked information or by uncommunicative press releases. The desire to keep secret world-wide processes of consultation among bishops and others in the Church is unrealistic. The Church must simply get used to the idea of working in the open, and this means dealing confidently and honestly with the press even in the early stages of decision making.

Church leaders need to be open with the faithful also. As *Communio et Progressio* clearly states, the Church is a living organism and it needs public opinion. Catholics must feel free to express their opinions, so that responsible dialogue can take place within the Church on matters of importance.[89] When research and analysis are commissioned by authority, their findings should not be buried in an embarrassed cover-up. When the faithful express a different point of view from their pastors, this should not be suppressed on the plea of 'not washing dirty linen in public'.

> There is an enormous area where members of the Church can express their views on domestic issues ... While the individual Catholic follows the *Magisterium*, he can and should engage in free research so that he may better understand revealed truths or explain them to a society subject to incessant change.[90]

The Catholic press has had a difficult time in Africa and other non-Western countries. Many Catholic newspapers and periodicals have foundered on the rock of editorial responsibility. One reason is because some bishops do not wish to see a diversity of views published. Moreover, they feel that any publication bearing the title 'Catholic' should reflect the *magisterium*. The idea of a free Catholic press in the hands of the laity is as repugnant to them as the idea of a free secular press is to certain authoritarian governments. They therefore exercise a form of censorship which, in the circumstances, is unnecessary, and which sometimes has the effect of torpedoing the project altogether. Evangelization is the responsibility of the whole people of God, and there is no reason why the use of the print media for evangelization should be monopolized by the clergy or hierarchy, or why the latter should be unduly sensitive about divergent views. Catholic newspapers and periodicals should be a platform for the responsible dialogue envisaged by the Vatican's pastoral instruction. Without an example of free dialogue within the Church, Christians cannot hope to correct the abuse of human freedoms in the secular sphere.

The laity are in need of attractive, sound and wholesome reading matter, and up to now the various Catholic printing presses and publishing houses have performed a valuable task. This is an apostolate which has to be pursued and expanded. Modern creative writers have usually been distinguished for their hostility towards, and criticism of, the Church. In spite of their popularity with the reading public, they are not as close to the grass roots as the Church they lampoon. Nevertheless, it is these anti-Christian works which are proposed as set texts for literature courses and examinations in non-Western schools and universities. The Church has sometimes – rightly – protested at the imposition of such texts, but the most effective counterweight would be to encourage creative writing which integrates, rather than opposes, Christian Gospel and traditional culture. A plea must also be made for students to become acquainted with great Christian works from other cultures.

Africa and other non-Western countries possess many traditional forms of communication which either survive in their original form, or which influence modern communications media. Most of them are relevant for what is called 'group media' or communication within and between local communities. The medium for which Africa is justly famous worldwide is dance. Whereas dance in the Western world tends to be a specialist performance intended for spectators, in Africa it is part of popular, social life. It accompanies song and is often dramatic in expression. Considerable emphasis is placed on dance in African schools, and creativity is encouraged through the formation of cultural groups and the holding of inter-school competitions. Banishing dance from the Christian liturgy is unnatural in Africa. If the Church is to be truly African, then it must encourage the development of liturgical dance.

Closely associated with dance is drama. Nothing is a more effective social commentary, a more powerful teaching aid, or a more expressive response to the Gospel than a dramatic performance. In its origins, drama all over the world is connected with religious worship, and it has only recently become secularized in the West. African traditions of drama are associated with rituals and with forms of spirit possession. Everywhere in Africa, people – especially young people – have a great love of drama. Drama is liturgically useful; it also serves to confer identity on the performing group. The same can be said for choirs and bands. As group media, such forms of communication help to express the ideals and values of a community and to teach them to the younger generation or to candidates for Christian initiation.

Story-telling is a traditional literary genre in non-Western cultures, together with other forms of oral tradition, such as proverbs, songs and riddles. Although it must compete nowadays with modern means of communication, it still survives in the family circle. Oral tradition has also influenced creative writing, film making, radio and television. Generally speaking, although technique has matched material in novel, film and radio, this has not been the case with television. It is clear that the Church must also make use of oral tradition in preaching, in creating catechetical material and in the self-expression of local communities. Sharing stories is an essential form of group activity. It can also be carried over into written and printed form. Although the production of parish magazines, and newsletters is a laborious business from which many pastoral teams shy away, they are invariably welcome to ordinary Christians. Such publications can be organized at the deanery or diocesan level, with space for parish additions which 'personalize' or particularize them. There are few more effective ways of promoting parish or community identity than through a publication.

Training and awareness

The superstructure for funding and training broadcasters, journalists and technicians already exists. The infrastructure, however, is not yet fully in place. Authorities must first be convinced of the necessity to make use of communications media, and to go in for production. Then there is a need for talent spotting. Speaking personally, I have tried, whenever possible, to encourage African writers and journalists, and to promote their work – if necessary, through co-authorship. As a missionary engaged in teaching and writing, I conceive this to be a duty. Talent spotting must, however, become a general concern in the Church, if inculturation is to become a reality and if any headway is to be made against the preponderance of Western media. As the late Fr Pedro Arrupe SJ pointed out in 1978, inculturation implies creativity.[91]

Talent spotting depends on awareness of needs and opportunities. At the moment the Catholic Church tries to create this awareness through the celebration of World Communications Sunday. The collection taken up on this day may be a small source of revenue for communications training and funding. As a vehicle for awareness and talent spotting the day may have a greater value. However, the celebration of World Communications Sunday does not appeal to many pastors. One reason is that the papal message for this day is often couched in technical vocabulary which is far from being a model of effective communication, and parish priests are not sure what the celebration is all about. Moreover, they may not welcome a specially prepared Mass which replaces the liturgy of the Sunday.

World Communications Sunday could, however, become an occasion for talent contests and for the presentation of group media in the parish. It could also be an opportunity for instructing parents about the modern media, offering them criteria of discernment in guiding their children's use of the media. It could even be an opportunity for making a contribution to the media through journalism or through a recorded dramatic or musical production. Essentially it should be a stimulus for creativity.

The root of the whole question, the problem with which we began this discussion, is: How do we make the modern means of communication a vehicle of inculturation? How can we turn what is essentially a vehicle of cultural alienation into one of valid inculturation? There is no simple answer to this question. All the angles we have considered here are part of the answer. It is abundantly clear, however, that the Church must not throw the weight of its authority and resources behind the process of alienation, but must help local Churches to use communications technology to promote their own cultural expression of the Gospel.

Redefining cultures

The richness of the world's cultural pluriformity is in imminent danger of being permanently devalued by a dominant technology and a secular outlook, emanating from the West. Rather than accept this alienating uniformity, it is being realized that indigenous non-Western cultures need to be redefined in the present situation. They can only do this by absorbing alien influences on their own terms, by reinterpreting them and by the creative and selective use of Western technology. Many observers are sceptical that such redefinition is possible, in the face of such an overwhelming cultural aggression, but the attempt should not be too quickly abandoned.

In earlier ages the Church came to the rescue of traditional culture. Christian monasteries preserved the cultural deposit of art, music and literature, and ecclesiastical patrons presided over successive movements of cultural renaissance. The Church did this for a supernatural reason, as much as for a natural one. Faith survived because it had become culture, and culture survived because it had become faith. The Church's interest in local culture stems from its commitment to evangelization. The Church is called upon to play the same role today and to uphold the religious and human values of local cultures in the power of the Gospel. It is called upon to do this on a worldwide scale. With the Church as an ally, the adepts of traditional cultures can look forward to some hope of success.

Unfortunately, it is not sure whether the Catholic Church is supportive or subversive of local cultures. In practice it promotes a cultural uniformity that is allied to the aggressive secularism of Europe and America. Although it has not succeeded in counteracting the forces of secularism and materialism in this culture, it clings blindly to the notion that it is still essentially Christian and that it should be a permanent component in the form which Christianity takes all over the world. The truth is that evangelization demands a commitment to local culture and a readiness to sacrifice the cultural forms of the West. Such a commitment requires a new model of Church and Church communion, which will be discussed in the next chapter.

A culturally polycentric Church is the only shape that Catholicism can take in the present situation, if evangelization itself is not to be compromised and the universality of the Church is not to be placed at risk. Inculturation is a vocation, a call, 'a task imposed' by Christ; and we have far to go towards its realization.[92] Inculturation is a constant call to cultural conversion, repeatedly answered in creative reinterpretations of culture and cultural re-expressions of the Gospel. On the necessity and urgency of inculturation praxis there is a remarkable consensus among theologians, and this conviction is gaining ground in the Church at large.

References

1 *L'Osservatore Romano* (28 June 1982), pp. 1–8.

2 Walbert Buhlmann, *With Eyes to See. The Church and the World in the Third Millennium* (Maryknoll, NY: Orbis Books, 1990) (originally published in German by Verlag Styria, 1989), p. 10.

3 One was the 1977 Swahili version (for Kenya) of the 1969 'All-Africa Eucharistic Prayer'. The other was the *Mtindo wa Ibada ya Misa kwa nchi ya Tanzania*, commissioned in 1975 and completed in 1977.

4 Letter from Archbishop James Komba of Songea, dated 5 August 1991, in the author's possession.

5 *L'Osservatore Romano*, n. 45 (7 November 1974), p. 9.

6 Ludwig Wittgenstein, *Philosophical Investigations* (Oxford: Blackwell, 1976), pp. 5, 12, 224.

7 Thierry G. Verhelst, *No Life Without Roots* (New York/London: Zed Books,

1990). Such creative reinterpretation is confusingly called 'inculturation' by this author.

8   Joseph Donders, 'Culture and Christian Development', *CAFOD Link* (Autumn 1990), issue 29, p. 4. Donders is reviewing Verhelst, op. cit., as well as my own *Toward a Theology of Inculturation* (London: Geoffrey Chapman/Maryknoll, NY: Orbis Books, 1988) in the same article; this is undoubtedly confusing, since the authors use the terms 'acculturation' and 'inculturation' differently.

9   Joseph Ratzinger (with V. Messori), *The Ratzinger Report* (Leominster: Fowler Wright, 1985), p. 103.

10 Donders proposes a seemingly unrealistic dialogue based on 'Kingdom principles' abstracted from their cultural form: Joseph G. Donders, 'Inculturation and Catholicity in Relation to the Worldwide Church', *Proceedings of the Catholic Theological Society of America*, vol. 45 (1990), p. 36. He also laments that the word 'dialogue' is not even found in the index to *Toward a Theology of Inculturation*, op. cit. Whatever the shortcomings of the index, inculturation is defined as 'dialogue' on pp. 11–12 and thereafter throughout the book. There is also a lengthy discussion of inter-faith dialogue on pp. 99–102.

11 Vincent Donovan, *Christianity Rediscovered* (London: SCM Press, 1978).

12 Ibid., p. 81.

13 It is pointed out by those familiar with the Maasai situation that Donovan's Christian communities were not, in fact, stable communities; they did not survive the missionary's departure from East Africa. Probably, the experiment was premature and more needs to be known about Maasai culture. (Personal communication from Franz Mol MHM.)

14 Donovan, op. cit., *passim*.

15 Paul Avis, *Christians in Communion* (London: Geoffrey Chapman Mowbray, 1990), p. 67.

16 Mary Tanner, 'Anglicans and the Ecumenical Future after Lambeth 1988', *One in Christ* (1989), vol. 25, no. 2, p. 133.

17 Avis, op. cit., p. vii.

18 Pedro Arrupe, 'Catechesis and Inculturation', *African Ecclesial Review*, vol. 20, no. 1 (1978), pp. 32–3.

19 *Sects or New Religious Movements – Pastoral Challenge* (Nairobi, 1985), pp. 17–18.

20 African Synod *Instrumentum Laboris*, 89. This passage does not occur in the chapter on inculturation, but in the chapter on dialogue.

21 Cf. Aylward Shorter, op. cit., p. 254; Roger Bastide, *The African Religions of Brazil* (Baltimore: Johns Hopkins University Press, 1978).

22 J.-Y. Calvez, 'The Real Problem of Inculturation', *Lumen Vitae*, vol. 40, no. 1 (1985), pp. 70–80.

23 K. O. Bimwenyi, 'Inculturation en Afrique et attitude des agents de l'évangelisation', *Bulletin of African Theology*, vol. 5 (1981), pp. 5–17 (author's trans.).

24 Cf. G. A. Arbuckle, *Earthing the Gospel* (London: Geoffrey Chapman/Maryknoll, NY: Orbis Books, 1990); another is N. Standaert, 'L'histoire d'un néologisme', *Nouvelle Revue Théologique*, no. 110 (1988), pp. 555–70.

25 *Evangelii Nuntiandi*, 63.

26 S. M. Michael, 'The Role of the Church in the Transformation of Culture', *Indian Missiological Review*, vol. 11, no. 1 (1989), pp. 75–95.

27 Calvez, op. cit., p. 72; Shorter, op. cit., pp. 17–30; Edmund Hill, 'Christianity and Cultures', *New Blackfriars*, vol. 67, nos 793/794 (1986), pp. 324–9.

28 P. Rottlander, 'One World: Opportunity or Threat for the Global Church?', *Concilium*, no. 204 (1989), p. 108.

29 J. B. Metz, 'Unity and Diversity: Problems and Prospects for Inculturation', *Concilium*, no. 204 (1989), p. 80; Aylward Shorter, *The Church in the African City* (London: Geoffrey Chapman/Maryknoll, NY: Orbis Books, 1991), *passim*.

30 Shorter, ibid.

31 D. S. Amalorpavadass, 'Réflexions théologiques sur l'inculturation', *La Maison Dieu*, no. 179 (1989), p. 58.

32 Rottlander, op. cit., p. 108; Metz, op. cit., p. 80.

33 Michael Drohan, 'Christianity, Culture and the Meaning of Mission', *International Review of Mission*, vol. 75, no. 299 (1986), pp. 298–9; cf. also Edmund Hill, op. cit., pp. 324–9, where Hill speaks of 'Christianity's all too successful inculturation in a violent, arrogant and aggressive culture' (p. 326).

34 Shorter, *Toward a Theology*, op. cit., p. 231; cf. also M. de C. Azevedo, *Inculturation and the Challenges of Modernity* (Rome: Pontifical Gregorian University Working Papers in Inculturation, 1982).

35 Metz, op. cit., p. 80.

36 Rottlander, op. cit., pp. 110–12.

37 Michael Amaladoss, 'Dialogue and Inculturation', *Inculturation*, no. 314 (1988), p. 24; Rottlander, op. cit., p. 113.

38 Metz, op. cit., p. 83.

39 Arrupe, op. cit., p. 32.

40 Arbuckle, op. cit.

41 Aidan Kavanagh, 'Liturgical Inculturation: Looking to the Future', *Studia Liturgica*, vol. 20 (1990), p. 98 (cf. also *La Maison Dieu*, no. 179 (1989), pp. 67–82, which gives a French version of the same paper, delivered to the 12th *Societas Liturgica* conference in York, 1989): 'You may still find me reactionary, but at least you will know more about what sort of reactionary I am . . .'

42 Kavanagh, 'Liturgical Inculturation', op. cit., p. 98.

43 Ibid., pp. 98–9.

44 Ratzinger (with Messori), op. cit., p. 103.

45 UCAN, AS7025/705 (9 March 1993).

46 Cf. Shorter, *Toward a Theology*, op. cit., pp. 183–6.

47 Gregory Baum, Introduction to *Concilium* 204 (1989), pp. xiv–xv.

48 To do him credit, this idea was explicitly abandoned by Cardinal Ratzinger in his address to the Asian Bishops. However, he has put forward the idea of a universal and permanent Western cultural matrix for evangelization.

49 *Evangelii Nuntiandi*, 63.

50 John M. Huels, 'Interpreting Canon Law in Diverse Cultures', *The Jurist*, vol. 47 (1987), p. 288; M. L. Stackhouse, 'Contextualization, Contextuality and Contextualism' in Ruy O. Costa (ed.), *One Faith – Many Cultures* (Maryknoll, NY: Orbis Books, 1988), pp. 3–13.

51 Robert J. Schreiter, *Constructing Local Theologies* (London: SCM Press, 1985), pp. 5–6; Amalorpavadass, op. cit., pp. 63–5; Stackhouse, op. cit., p. 6.

52 Clifford Geertz, 'Religion as a Cultural System' in M. Banton (ed.), *Anthropological Approaches to the Study of Religion* (London: Tavistock Publications, 1966), pp. 1–46.

53 Stackhouse, op. cit., p. 8.

54 F. R. de Gasperis, 'Community and the Newness of Faith in the Mother Church of Jerusalem' in P. Beauchamp *et al.* (eds), *Bible and Inculturation* (Rome, 1983), p. 60; Calvez, op. cit., p. 77; Schreiter, op. cit., pp. 5–6.

55 Standaert, op. cit., p. 564.

56 International Theological Commission, 'Faith and Culture', *Omnis Terra*, no. 198 (1989), p. 265.

57 Casimir Guanadickam, 'Inculturation and the Local Church', *Lumen Vitae*, vol. 40, no. 1 (1985), p. 67, quoting *L'Osservatore Romano* of 9 January 1983.

58 Standaert, op. cit., p. 564.

59 Standaert, ibid.; *Evangelii Nuntiandi*, 63.

60 Adrian Hastings, 'Western Christianity Confronts Other Cultures', *Studia Liturgica*, vol. 20, no. 1 (1990), pp. 24–5; Arbuckle, op. cit., pp. 190–1.

61 Kavanagh, op. cit., p. 105; cf. John Paul II's Address to the Zaïrean Bishops in 1980, *African Ecclesial Review*, vol. 22, no. 4 (1980), pp. 4–5, in which he implied that inculturation in African could take as many centuries as in Poland.

62 Cf. J. M. Waliggo, 'Making a Church That Is Truly African' in J. M. Waliggo *et al.* (eds), *Inculturation: Its Meaning and Urgency* (Nairobi, 1986), pp. 11–30; and J. Mutiso-Mbinda, 'Inculturation: Challenge to the Local Church', ibid., p. 76.

63 *Lineamenta* of African Synod, chap. 2, no. 51. My italics.

64 Metz, op. cit., p. 86.

65 Titus Pressler, 'Christianity Rediscovered: A Reflection on Vincent Donovan's Contribution to Missiology', *Missiology*, vol. 18, no. 3 (1990), p. 272.

66 Hill, op. cit., p. 328; Albert Nolan, *God in South Africa* (London: CIIR, 1988), *passim*; Shorter, *Toward a Theology*, op. cit., pp. 59–63.

67 Shorter, ibid., pp. 64–5.

68 Ibid., pp. 65–7.

69 *Evangelii Nuntiandi*, 63, 64.

70 W. Reiser, 'Inculturation and Doctrinal Development', *Heythrop Journal*, vol. 22 (1981), p. 137.

71 Calvez, op. cit., p. 73; Rottlander, op. cit., p. 112; Metz, op. cit., p. 79.

72 Kavanagh, op. cit., p. 104.

73 Angel Anton, 'The Theological Status of Episcopal Conferences' in Hervé Legrand *et al.* (eds), *The Nature and Future of Episcopal Conferences* (Washington, DC: Catholic University of America Press, 1988), pp. 185–219.

74 Anton, op. cit., p. 202.

75 Reiser, op. cit., p. 136; cf. *Lumen Gentium*, 23; *Ad Gentes Divinitus*, 22.

76 Anton, op. cit., pp. 193ff.

77 Cf. the 'Apostolate to the Nomads' in eastern Africa which unites dioceses in seven different countries.

78   Jesus Hortal, 'Relations among Episcopates' in Legrand *et al.*, op. cit., pp. 174–80.
79   Michel Legrain, 'Young Churches and the New Code of Canon Law', *Theology Digest*, vol. 31 (1984), p. 217.
80   Ibid., p. 218.
81   Steven Bwana, 'The Impact of the New Code in Africa', *Concilium* no. 185 (1986), pp. 103–9; Kurt Piskaty, 'The Process of Contextualization and Its Limits', *Verbum SVD*, vol. 24 (1983), pp. 163–71; Legrain, op. cit., p. 218.
82   Piskaty, op. cit., p. 170–1.
83   Efoé-Julien Pénoukou, *Églises d'Afrique: Propositions pour l'Avenir* (Paris: 1984), discusses the role of the local bishop as guarantor of inculturation; see also Shorter, *Toward a Theology*, op. cit., p. 194.
84   Shorter, ibid., pp. 251–4; 261–71.
85   L. Ngakane and K. Shiri, *Africa on Film* (London: BBC Publications, 1991).
86   Michael E. Williams, 'The Media (*Inter Mirifica*)' in Adrian Hastings (ed.), *Modern Catholicism – Vatican II and After* (London: SPCK/New York: OUP, 1991), p. 169.
87   The meeting was held at Villa Cavalletti, Frascati, in 1983. It was sponsored by the Society of Jesus.
88   *Communio et Progressio*, 114–125.
89   Ibid., 115–121.
90   Ibid., 117.
91   Pedro Arrupe, 'Letter to the Whole Society on Inculturation' (1978) in J. Aixala (ed.), *Other Apostolates Today: Selected Letters and Addresses of Pedro Arrupe SJ* (St Louis: Institute of Jesuit Sources, 1981), p. 172.
92   Hill, op. cit., p. 328.

5 An evangelization model of Church

Power of love versus love of power

The greatest commandment of the law, according to Jesus, is to love God above all and one's neighbour as oneself (Matt 22:34–40; Mark 12:28–34; Luke 10:25–28). His 'new' commandment is to love one another, as he has loved us (John 13:31–35; 15:12–13). This commandment provides the impulse of evangelization. In fact, it is a movement towards Trinitarian oneness, towards a union with God of all those he loves (John 17:20–23). As Jesus foretold, this love has the power to attract people. Love makes us want to be poor with the poor and other with the other. The power of love is sacrifice, and Jesus contrasted this with the love of power. The greatest among his followers would be the last of all, like a servant, or a child, but unlike the heathen rulers who enjoyed exercising power over others (Matt 20:25–28). 'The Son of man came not to be served, but to serve and to give his life as a ransom for many.'

The community which Jesus left behind him to carry out his mission was to be distinguished by this quality of sacrificial love, and to be moved by its power to evangelize the world. Such love would identify people as his followers. Christ's Church was not intended to be a power phenomenon, or an instrument of control. Although the community was in need of leadership and regulation, these were to be exercised by example, counsel and service, not by the kind of coercion, legalism and retribution which characterized the opponents of Jesus. The Church is the seed and beginning of a spiritual Kingdom, the reign of God, and it is called to develop in conformity with the Kingdom's demands. The Church strives ceaselessly to be worthy of the Kingdom it proclaims.

It is understandable that the love of power should sometimes be a temptation in the Church, just as it was among the apostles themselves. Although the Church, because of its divine head, is unfailingly holy, it is also a pilgrim Church that receives its perfection only in heaven.[1] It is in constant need of reformation and renewal, because its members are sinful. It is in the nature of an organization marked by the sins and failures of its members sometimes to limit its horizons, to adopt particular political causes and systems, even to identify exclusively with a particular continent or culture. The Church of every epoch must reflect on how well it is carrying out the mission entrusted to it, how well it is performing its function as sacrament of the world, how successful it is in revealing the presence of Christ and co-operating with the activity of his Spirit in every corner of the world, and in every shape or form of human experience. In other words, it must be a constant point of self-examination to ask: How Catholic is the Church?

The Church's vocation of Catholicity is bound up with its duty of evangelization/inculturation. Its love embraces the whole of humanity and its message is addressed to the whole world. The deepest desire of the Church is not to colonize others, to impose alien cultural traditions on them or to violate the human right to an authentic culture. Its profound wish is to enter into other cultural worlds, other mentalities, other systems of human thought and behaviour, and to uphold them in the power of the Gospel, which is the power of love and truth. Through the Good News, the Church desires to make these cultural traditions more genuine and more true, if that were possible, to their own original insights. Through the power of Christ's love, these cultures can be raised to a new and more glorious life. Their destiny in the Church is not to be despised, let alone submerged or destroyed.

The contemporary malaise in the Catholic Church

People like myself who travel, and who encounter different groups of laity, religious and priests in the course of their work, are aware of a malaise in the Roman Catholic Church today. These people love the Church and are deeply loyal to it. They are patient and optimistic Christians, but they suffer deeply. The pain is widespread, and is caused by the feeling that there is something seriously wrong. They recognize that the Church in every age is marked by the sin of its members, and is, in the words of Karl Rahner, a 'sinful Church', but they feel that the wrong which afflicts today's Church has a special intensity that is causing embarrassment and pain to the most faithful among them.[2]

The feeling of unhappiness centres on the totalitarian manner in which authority is sometimes understood and exercised in the Church. It is a type of authority that encourages fear and distrust, and it filters down to the lowest levels of the Church, stifling local initiatives, encouraging a top-down approach, manipulating appointments and discouraging efforts in the field of inculturation. This understanding of authority relies on the detection and condemnation of 'enemies within'. It operates through manipulation and secret denunciation, and assumes that freedom of communication in the Church is incompatible with the role of the Church's teaching authority. With sadness, these people remark the extraordinary power accorded to pressure-groups and organizations which have a narrow, one-sided and legalistic ecclesiology.

Pope John XXIII called the Second Vatican Council to carry out positive, rather than punitive, reforms. There were to be no anathemas, he said, and this was in line with the Pope's preference for what he called 'the medicine of mercy', rather than condemnation.[3] This is entirely in line with the spirit and practice of Jesus himself, who denounced sin but refused to condemn the sinner. 'Neither do I condemn you', said Jesus to the woman caught in the act of adultery, 'Go and do not sin any more' (John 8:11). The feeling is that the Church is in danger of relapsing into the language and practice of condemnation and anathema.

Equally devastating is the habit of raising unfounded hopes. Consultations are carried out and the resulting advice is seemingly set aside. The suspicion takes root that consultation is a sham, and that the distinction between consultation and deliberation is dubious. There is also, apparently, a growing gap between teaching and practice – something that is particularly clear in the case of inculturation. All of this undermines the credibility of authority. Furthermore, the assumption is made that the existence of past Christian cultures (Christendom) in Euro-America gives Westerners a permanent right to dominate the rest of the Church. Moreover, Euro-American wealth and know-how are used to steal the initiative from non-Western local Churches.

A serious implementation of inculturation which would allow local Churches to live and express their Christian faith distinctively and differently is being obstructed or indefinitely postponed. The so-called 'young Churches' are not thought ready for inculturation. As a result, it is possible that inculturation will go underground and that Catholic unity will be jeopardized.

It is too often said that the Catholic Church is not a democracy. That is certainly true, but why should it continue to be a feudal monarchy? The collegiate character of the Church's hierarchy under the headship of the Pope requires it to settle matters of major importance 'conjointly'.[4] Surely the mode in which it operates could draw on contemporary democratic practice, just as it borrowed feudal structures in the feudal age? No doubt the Church's faith-statements should derive from the consensus of its teaching authority, reflected in the *sensus fidelium*, and not from parliamentary lobbying, debate and division. However, democratic freedom, which is a principle of the Church's own social teaching, offers other lessons, especially that of accountability within a system of checks and balances. If the Catholic Church operated a more open and accountable system of government and decision-making, we might have been spared some of the financial and other scandals which have recently sullied the Church's reputation.

There are many voices calling for more democracy of this kind in the Church, and especially that the Church's social principles of solidarity and subsidiarity be applied to the Church's own life. This means principally that lay people should be given a greater share in the governing and decision-making processes, even if the ultimate responsibility for these activities, in addition to teaching and liturgical leadership, rests with the hierarchy and their clerical co-operators. The Church needs to empower lay people – men and women – to contribute at different levels and in different ways to the common task of the whole People of God.

These ideas are not new. They are to be found in the documents of the Second Vatican Council. Many of them are clearly expressed in the 1971 Synodal Document on Justice in the World. This document was accepted by Paul VI and published by him, but the bishops' recommendations have not been convalidated in their entirety. Among them we find the basic need for the Church to witness to justice in its own life and practice. Everyone, including women, has a right to be heard in a spirit of dialogue, and all members of the Church should have some share in decision-making, especially in the councils which should be set up at all levels.[5] The bishops were thinking especially of the diocesan pastoral council, which Vatican II recommended, and to which *Ecclesiae Sanctae* attributed a merely consultative role.[6]

Evangelization, therefore, calls for a healing of the contemporary Church. It must be restored to full health and made whole. It must become a more obvious sign and seed of God's Kingdom, of Trinitarian oneness and love, 'so that the world may believe' (John 17:21). This should be one of the objectives of the Decade of Evangelization. Pope John Paul II, echoing Paul VI, declared in *Redemptoris Missio*: 'Modern man puts more faith in a witness than in a teacher; he prefers experience to teaching, life and action to theory'.[7] Effective evangelization, therefore, demands such a witness. Through its life and action, the Christian community attracts others to join it. Modern people are not attracted by old-fashioned judgemental attitudes and condemnations, still less by manipulation and subterfuge. They are repelled by authoritarianism, power-play and alien cultural domination, and so they should be. These are not Gospel principles. The exercise of authority in today's Church demands openness and love, attitudes which invite solidarity and offer co-responsibility. Those who join the Catholic Church should be welcomed for the gifts they bring to the community, and should look forward to the exercise of responsibility in it.

The exercise of human power commonly implies the victimization of the poor and weak by the rich and powerful. It also connotes the stigmatization of the poor and weak, because the rich and powerful justify their domination by appealing to their own moral and spiritual superiority. The poor exist (so it is thought) to be ruled, and are judged incapable of superior thoughts or feelings. Every theory of hierarchy, caste, class or rank is based on perceived distinctions of this kind. The exercise of power rests on superordination and subordination. The mark of paganism is to identify God with the rich and powerful, to claim the moral high ground for those who dominate and lord it over others.

The revolutionary teaching of Christ is that God identifies with the poor and weak, and that the Kingdom belongs to them. Christ's kingship is not of this world. It is not a question of worldly power; rather it is the exercise of sacrificial love and service in the community. Christian mission and ministry derive from the selfsame love, and from the conviction that God speaks with the voice of the poor. Those who serve in the Church do so, not because they are holier, wiser, stronger or more knowledgeable than others, but because the community needs their service and, through its leaders, confers upon them a share in Christ's ministry, setting them apart to do the work to which they are called by the Spirit (Acts 13:2). There is therefore a strict relationship between ministry and the community, but ministry exists for the sake of the community, not vice versa.

It follows that the contemporary Church needs to undergo a profound conversion. Even more than this, a new model of Church must be born. It must be a model in which the experience of community is basic. The new paradigm of a *koinonia* Church must be genuinely and wholeheartedly adopted. In practice, this also means a culturally polycentric Church. This is a necessary condition for the success of the current Decade of Evangelization, and especially for the 'new evangelization'. The Church needs to reshape its institutions and structures, so that they can really be effective instruments of evangelization in the third millennium.

A new model of Church

In a Church communion characterized by true *koinonia* and mutual ministry, it is essential that the relationships between the local Churches be on an equal footing. It is clear, of course, that the Bishop of Rome has a 'concern for all the Churches' (2 Cor 11:28) and exercises immediate, universal jurisdiction, but that is not to say that every local Church should become a carbon copy of the local Church of Rome of which he is Bishop. There is a *de facto* inequality between local Churches. On the one hand, local Churches of the non-Western world have burgeoning populations. Their numbers of baptized and of vocations are growing and their religious fervour is remarkable, but they lack material resources. On the other hand, the local Churches of the Western world are declining both in numbers and in fervour, but their members are affluent and they dispose of sums that transcend the wildest dreams of Third World Christians.

In practice, many non-Western local Churches are materially dependent on the Church in the West. This is particularly true of Africa, less so of Latin America, where Church leaders enjoy relatively more freedom. Effective power in the Church, therefore, lies with the West, because centralized authority is located there and because this is backed by material wealth. Wittingly or unwittingly the Catholic Church duplicates the socio-economic reality of a world ruled by an affluent white minority regime. No doubt the superfluous wealth of the West should be channelled into the poorer regions of the earth, but not at the expense of the relative autonomy which belongs by right to local Church communities. Bishops and Church leaders find it difficult not to be subservient to this Eurocentric pattern of centralization and uniformity.

If centralization in the Church were really thoroughgoing, it would be intolerable. It would amount to a form of cultural imperialism and thought control which would be counter-productive from a Christian point of view. In point of fact, it operates inefficiently and selectively, but it has the unfortunate effect of producing the kind of Church leader who is cowed into public submission, while expressing private opinions that are more palatable to the local Church community. There are many obvious ways in which local Churches can develop their own spontaneous expressions of faith, worship, ministry and Christian life independently of centralized authority, especially at the grass roots. The tragedy is that Eurocentrism and over-centralization often make it difficult for bishops to provide leadership and to recognize local initiative, and there is a danger that grass roots Catholicism may grow in a different direction. This threat to Catholic unity was foreseen by the late Fr Pedro Arrupe in 1977, and was noted in the last chapter.

It is difficult not to succumb to the temptation of manipulating others when one holds the purse-strings, yet the holiness of the Church and its vocation to live up to the demands of the Kingdom require that the temptation be resisted. Local Churches may not be economically viable. They may also have an ongoing need of personnel from elsewhere, but they must not be judged 'immature', 'young' or 'junior' on that account. If they are deemed to be a local Church at all, they must be given immediate equality of status. Their freedom of action and responsibility must be scrupulously safeguarded.

The communion of local Churches which constitutes the Catholic Church is guaranteed by – indeed centred on – the Petrine office. Communion with the See of Peter is what makes a local Church the Catholic Church of that locality. From the point of view of hierarchical ministry, Catholic communion is monocentric. It has a single centre or focus. However, from the point of view of culture, Catholic communion is by definition polycentric. This means having as many cultural centres as there are viable local cultures. It also means that the language of communion should not be monopolized by any single culture, not even that of the Pope's own diocese.

A culturally polycentric Church, a *koinonia* Church, is a Church that is really convinced of the value of dialogue. It is a Church convinced that evangelization is a two-way, not a one-way, process. It is a Church that recognizes its Master's voice when he speaks from other cultures and faith traditions, particularly when he speaks with the voice of the poor. It is a Church that believes he has a message for the evangelizer, as much as for the evangelized. It is a Church that is humble enough to reflect deeply on its encounter with 'otherness', and even to rethink the formulation of its own message in the light of this encounter.

Doctrine and theology in a culturally polycentric Church

Modern biblical scholarship has taught us the importance of the early Christian communities in the formulation of the Christian faith tradition. The New Testament is evidence for previously existing oral traditions and for a narrative memory of Jesus which was the property of a number of early Christian communities.[8] The two consequences of accepting the primacy of the early Christian communities are that the formulation of the one faith is subject to progressive development and that, secondly, it is a pluralistic phenomenon.[9] By and large, the idea that there should be a single interpretation, or a single theology, in the Church has been an illusion. Theological pluralism, as Bernard Lonergan pointed out, is primarily a pluralism of communication rather than of doctrine, but there is no communication of doctrine 'except through the rituals, narrative forms, titles, parables and metaphors that are effective in the given (cultural) milieu'.[10] A culturally polycentric Church is a Church identified with an empirically perceived pluralism. It is a Church that accepts a plurality of understandings, applications and expressions of Catholic teaching that are consistent with the meaning of its historic faith-statements. It does not wish to impose a total uniformity of understanding, application and expression on theology, let alone on the day-to-day teaching and preaching of doctrine. It is happy to leave the door open where there is room for further discussion. Moreover, it does not believe that doctrinal development is unilinear. As we have already seen, the discernment of a succession of paradigms seems to present a truer picture of the reality.

In a culturally polycentric or *koinonia* Church, the papal *magisterium* would work in closer harmony with the local *magisterium*. Without denying the right of the Pope (solemnly defined by Vatican I) to address the whole Church as universal shepherd and teacher, especially when it is a question of making infallible definitions of dogma, or of offering guidance on questions that affect the world as a whole, much of the ordinary papal teaching would be delegated to the local bishops. The Pope would provide the general principles and necessary guidance, but it would be up to the local bishops to draft their own texts and apply the principles to their own concrete situations. According to its constitution, the Pope can already give the Synod of Bishops deliberative power, if he chooses, and this would, no doubt, be the norm in a culturally polycentric Church. The primacy would then be exercised in a context of collegiality, rather than the reverse. Moreover, synodal documents would try to reflect more scrupulously the variety of interpretation and practice current in the Church.

More than this, a central mechanism would have to be created through which the *magisterium* of the particular Churches could be shared and made available. In this way, the teachings and pastoral initiatives of local bishops could mutually invigorate the local Churches.[11] Already an attempt is being made to bring together the social teaching of the local bishops, and this is an obvious field of interest.[12] Writing on inculturation sometimes exhibits a somewhat static understanding of culture, and even a mechanistic picture of the intercultural process. It is important to realize that cultures do genuinely interact, and do borrow and learn from one another. The universal communion of the Church should facilitate this intercultural action (interculturation), without encouraging bias toward any one particular culture, and without usurping local cultural autonomy.

The new *Catechism of the Catholic Church* offers an interesting further case in point. It has been presented to the universal Church as a comprehensive summary of Catholic doctrinal and moral teaching. However, its cultural limitations are recognized. Although it will be available in European-language translations for Catholics to read all over the world, it is primarily intended as a catechetical source book and guide for local bishops to use. However, a debate is already taking place about how far bishops are permitted to go in their selection and adaptation of this material for catechetical use in their own cultural milieux. Even the Bible needs to be understood in the light of its manifold texts and contexts, its literary genres and the hierarchy of truths it proposes. All these have to be explained to people in modern situations that are culturally alien to those of the Bible, before they can shed light on God's present action in the community. Surely, considerably less, rather than more, should be claimed for the new catechism than is claimed for the inspired Word of God?

Pope John Paul II's words, already quoted above, are an unanswerable argument against the fantasy of a Christian world culture. 'A faith which does not become culture is a faith which has not been fully received, not thoroughly thought through, not fully lived out.'[13] The language of faith is always that of the evangelized culture, and attempts to impose a universal language result in a superficial standardization that at best appears culture-bound and irrelevant, and at worst encourages syncretism.[14] This is the dilemma of every 'universal' document issuing from a centralized *magisterium* to the lived pluralism of the Church: from typical editions of liturgical books, apostolic exhortations and encyclical letters to a universal Code of Canon Law and the text of a universal catechism.

Even in the realm of theology, while we have already – by and large – conceded the existence of a plurality of theologies, we still gratuitously assume a uniform concept of theology itself.[15] All that can be realistically achieved at the macro-level is to develop what Metz has called theological 'bridging categories' and operate a 'cross-cultural hermeneutic'.[16] The development of such a hermeneutic is the task of authority, operating at the level of world communion. It is a complex and delicate exercise of collegiality and co-responsibility by which a central resource centre (perhaps a revamped International Theological Commission) can help local Churches understand what each other is saying and learn new interests from one another, while defining the bounds of legitimate diversity. The operation of a cross-cultural hermeneutic will constitute a guide to the right understanding of tradition, as well as a vehicle for correct cultural translation. It goes without saying that it would need to be multilingual and multicultural. It cannot be anchored in, or identified with, any one language or culture.

The law and structures of culturally polycentric communion

Law, as opposed to legalism, is both healthy and necessary in the Church. It upholds people's rights and defines their duties. The new model of Church communion, however, cannot tolerate a universal Canon Law that reflects an outmoded paradigm of mission. The new model is inconsistent with an invasive law that subverts local cultures, produces cultural parallelism, or contributes to an ongoing cultural aggression by the West. As matters stand now, the universal law of the Church is used as an instrument for blocking effective evangelization and hindering the progress of inculturation. Obviously, this must be changed in a culturally polycentric Church.

The 1983 Code of Canon Law incorporates many pastoral insights from the Second Vatican Council. Moreover, it offers local Churches many different options for applying the law. Episcopal conferences, lacking the expertise and unused to taking such initiatives, have been slow to make use of the opportunities which the new code affords. However, in the final analysis, the possibility of variation is insufficient. Canon Law remains a unified code that reflects its Western culture of origin and assumes that the Church is culturally monolithic. The new model of Church requires a new kind of Canon Law. Vatican II recommended local adaptations in the field of ecclesiastical legislation.[17] Canonists like Michel Legrain have taken up this suggestion and called for a central legal framework or *loi-cadre*, within which local Churches could formulate their own codes.[18] This was also the recommendation of the Secretaries-General of African Episcopal Conferences, meeting at the Fifth SECAM Plenary in Nairobi in 1978, who asked for an African Code of Canon Law.[19] Unfortunately, all such suggestions were overtaken by the 1983 Code, which was designed as a uniform law for the whole Church.

The Church's law, as currently formulated, is one of the greatest obstacles to the realization of inculturation. What is needed is a system of law that facilitates, rather than impedes, inculturation. However, this assumes that local hierarchies have the self-confidence and the trained personnel to create and apply a locally inculturated legislation. Under the provisions of the 1983 Code, local hierarchies are empowered to establish their own tribunals and courts of appeal, but these opportunities are not adequately taken up because trained personnel are often lacking. The new model of Church requires a fully developed local structure which makes the benefits of the law available to everyone in the Church, and which interprets the law according to local, rather than foreign, juridical realities.

The Vatican diplomatic service is a valuable instrument of Catholic communion. There are many instances in recent history where it has stepped in to rescue a local Church from government persecution or discrimination. The international outreach of the Roman Catholic Church is one of its great strengths, and the device of a diplomatic service, however anomalous and ambivalent the representation of the tiny Vatican State may be, is a considerable asset. The Vatican State is a collection of ancient buildings on the edge of a garden in the centre of Rome. It is entirely dependent on the good will and co-operation of the Italian state in which it is situated. Its representatives, the nuncios and delegates, are more occupied with Church business than with the secular interests that concern the host governments to which they are accredited. Clearly, they are valuable adjuncts of the papal ministry. Obviously too, they assume a greater profile in the poorer countries of the non-Western world.

In a new model of Church, these Vatican diplomats would place a greater emphasis on representing the local Churches to the Holy See. They would be more multinational and missionary in character, ready to espouse the language, culture and ethos of the country they serve. Their terms of competence with regard to the local episcopal conference and the local government would be carefully circumscribed, so that there would be less likelihood of a clash of interests. If Vatican diplomats are agents of the Pope's universal jurisdiction, they must also guard against any suspicion that they are infringing the freedom of action of the local Church.[20]

In the new Church model Canon Law would make provisions for deliberative particular councils at regional international levels. Such councils would be held *cum Petro et sub Petro*, that is to say, under the aegis of the Pope and subject to his ratification, though not necessarily in his presence or on his initiative. Such councils are well known in the history of the Church, but they do not figure in the 1983 Code of Canon Law. The 'Special Assembly for Africa of the Synod of Bishops' illustrates this point rather well.[21] It is sixteen years since the idea of an African Council 'on African soil' was first proposed by priests and laity, members of the African Society for Culture, and thirteen years since the bishops of Zaïre first raised the matter with the Pope. The logic behind the proposal was that the celebration of a particular council on African soil would give the lie to those who claim that Christianity in Africa is foreign, and that the African Church is still under Western tutelage. It would allow the African Church to decide its own pastoral agenda and would evoke the memory of the great African Councils of the early Church.

During the long years of debate about the character and appropriateness of such a meeting, the initial concept of a particular council was gradually made to conform to the requirements of the 1983 Code of Canon Law. It followed that, when Pope John Paul II finally made the project his own early in 1989, it took the shape of a Special Assembly of the Synod of Bishops. In this guise, it fell under the control of the Synod's secretariat, assisted by a specially constituted preparatory commission. In July 1990 the *Lineamenta*, or outline discussion paper of the Synod, was handed to the All-Africa Bishops' Symposium in Lomé, which was asked to carry the discussion down to the grass roots.

In 1993, during the Pope's visit to Uganda, the Synod's *Instrumentum Laboris*, or working paper, was promulgated, and it was announced that the working session of the Synod would be held in 1994, not on African soil as had been hoped, but in Rome where all previous Synods of Bishops had taken place. Although the working paper was drawn up by African bishops, priests and theologians and although it made use of responses coming from 31 African episcopal conferences, its methodology consisted in deductions from papal teaching and their application to Africa, rather than the inductive examination of African realities and the evaluation of them in the light of the *magisterium*.[22] In this example, we see how the initial process was reversed, and how an idea that arose in Africa was handed back from Rome in a different form.

The African Synod may occasion far-reaching reflection and may achieve practical and beneficial results for the Church in that continent, but in its present form it represents a lost opportunity and a turning away from the model of a *koinonia* Church. The structures of such a Church, however, do not yet exist. Canon Law which is the expression of a particular ecclesiology necessarily lags behind the developing ecclesial reality, and runs the risk of being used to slow down or impede the development itself. The positive options of the 1983 Code should, on the contrary, be used to the full and its diversity of application maximized, so that its limitations may become more conspicuous, and the need for a new, diversified system of law more keenly felt.

Liturgical inculturation in the *koinonia* Church

In the early Church a number of worship traditions or 'rites' developed out of the interaction of the various ecclesial communities with their diverse cultural environments. In the East a number of Oriental rites came into existence, but in the West a single Roman rite was carried by Latin missionaries to the illiterate pagans of northern Europe, displacing even the ancient traditions of contemporary Celtic missionaries. Adaptation took the invariable form of functional substitution. Pagan sacred places, seasons and rituals were simply replaced by Roman Christian ones.[23] The Roman rite enjoyed the prestige of a literary, artistic and technologically superior culture, and although eventually local variations appeared, such as the Ambrosian rite in Milan, the Mozarabic rite in Spain and the Sarum rite in England, it retained a monolithic homogeneity which was unchallenged.

The Protestant Reformation, which advocated vernacular liturgies and Bible translations, represented a radical diversification which threatened this relative homogeneity. The response of the Catholic Counter-Reformation was to halt all trends towards pluriformity, to impose a massive standardization and to abolish all liturgical usages less than two hundred years old. This occurred tragically at the very moment when sixteenth-century Latin missionaries were on the verge of discovering new cultures and faiths in the Americas, Africa, Asia and the Far East. Controversy followed upon the Jesuits' attempts to evangelize ancient oriental cultures from within. Ricci in China and de Nobili in India provided striking precedents for Propaganda Fide's policy of respect for the secular aspects of other cultures.[24] Unfortunately, no serious attempt was made to implement the policy, which would indeed have proved unworkable anyway, since the religious and secular aspects of culture cannot be so easily separated. In any case, there was no question of introducing culturally diverse liturgies.

Modern liturgical inculturation takes its origin in the movement precipitated by the Vatican II Constitution on the Sacred Liturgy, *Sacrosanctum Concilium*, and in the establishment by Paul VI of the liturgical Consilium which oversaw the revision of liturgical books. The crucial step was to allow the use of the vernacular in the Roman liturgy. This entailed a massive worldwide exercise of translation and also encouraged a formidable burst of creativity in producing musical settings for the new texts. Indeed, the work of translation was seen as foreshadowing a later, more creative phase of liturgical adaptation.[25]

Although the liturgical constitution provided for 'legitimate variations and adaptations', the 'substantial unity' of the Roman rite was to be preserved.[26] It was unfortunate, moreover, that the constitution was drawn up before the Council discussed the nature of the Church and human culture in *Lumen Gentium* and *Gaudium et Spes*. Its lack of an anthropological background is also serious.[27] This made it easier for a reaction to set in after the departure of Cardinal Lercaro, Archbishop Bugnini and the first members of the Consilium. From the mid-1970s liturgical creativity was frozen and the revision of the liturgy virtually became a new instrument of standardization.

In the 1990s a liturgical expert, Anscar Chupungco, is able to define liturgical inculturation as no more than 'dynamic translation', although he contemplates the remote possibility of a further phase of 'liturgical creativity'.[28] In other words, creativity is seen as the prerogative of a central authority, periodically exercised. Liturgical activity all over the world is basically 'translation'. This explains the preoccupation with texts, their submission to, and judgement by, Rome. The 'dynamism' of translation consists in a superficial adaptation. Chupungco's view accurately describes the present situation in the Roman Catholic Church, but it represents a serious misunderstanding of inculturation, which is essentially creative.

In its Decree on the Oriental Churches, *Orientalium Ecclesiarum*, the Second Vatican Council offered a more mature view of liturgical diversity. It stated that the Church wishes the traditions of each particular Church or rite to remain 'whole and entire', and it went on to say that the Church 'wishes to adapt its own way of life to the needs of different times and places'.[29] The Oriental rites were therefore examples of the way in which the Church adapts to different contexts. When Paul VI delivered the first address of his journey to Africa in 1969, he asked: 'Must the Church be European, Latin, Oriental ... or must she be African?' The summary of his answer is that in Africa the Church must be African as well as Catholic.[30] But did the Pope really mean to put the African Church on an equal footing with the Latin and Oriental Churches? If he did, he was far from realistic.

Africa has been evangelized by Western missionaries of Roman or Latin rite. Although a Catholic Coptic rite and a Catholic Ethiopic rite have been created on the model of the existing Orthodox Coptic and Ethiopic rites, the suggestion by Boniface Luykx in the mid-1970s that they might become a model for sub-Saharan Africa was never taken up.[31] It is clear that liturgical creativity in black Africa must build on the foundations of the Roman rite. This, in fact, is what has happened, as the examples of the Ndzon Melen Mass in Cameroun, the All-Africa Eucharistic Prayer and the Zaïre Mass have shown.

The Ndzon Melen liturgy makes no change of order or text. It is simply a manner of celebrating the Roman rite. However, the brightly coloured vestments and voluminous robes worn by ministers, servers, singers and dancers, together with the extensive choreography throughout the celebration, make it a visual and emotional experience very far removed from that of a Sunday Mass in Europe or North America.[32] There can be few celebrations in which priests are required to execute elaborate dance-steps while incensing the altar, for example. Ndzon Melen is a more elaborate version of many ordinary parish liturgies in Africa, with their choreographed entrance, readers' and offertory processions, their dramatized readings, responses and incidental gestures and postures. In such celebrations, the sober Eucharistic prayer from the Roman Missal often appears even more anticlimactic.

The so-called All-Africa Eucharistic Prayer was composed at Gaba Pastoral Institute shortly after Paul VI's visit to Uganda in July–August 1969. Its occasion was the verbal encouragement given, during a visit to Gaba, by Archbishop Annibale Bugnini, Secretary of the Congregation for Divine Worship, and it owed much to a seminar on African traditional prayer. The aim was to produce a discussion text which embodied characteristic African values and themes culled from the recorded prayer literature of non-Christian traditions. These included such concepts as the veneration of ancestors, kinship, fecundity, the blood-pact, the festal meal and the personalization of mysteries. The style was responsorial. The prayer did not, therefore, arise from a given ethnic cultural context, although certain sections were directly inspired by particular prayer texts. In spite of this weakness, the prayer had a more universal appeal than it would have done if it had been tied more closely to a particular ethnic culture.

The All-Africa Eucharistic Prayer was published early in 1970 and almost immediately appeared in French.[33] It was used in unauthorized celebrations in East, West and South Africa, and a Swahili version was prepared in 1977 at the request of the bishops of Kenya, who wished to submit it for approval. It was not, however, adopted. Three years later, shortly before the appearance of *Eucharistiae Participationem*, three more African Eucharistic Prayers were composed at Gaba and published in 1973. These were called 'Kenyan', 'Tanzanian' and 'Ugandan' and were more closely linked to traditional ethnic prayer models in each of the three countries. For this reason, they were more successful compositions in themselves, and, although they did not attract the wide interest generated by the All-Africa Eucharistic Prayer, they were more favourably received by liturgical specialists.[34] One critic, himself, eventually proposed an Igbo Eucharistic Prayer from Nigeria.[35]

These early initiatives were soon overtaken by a new Eucharistic rite from Zaïre, which may have owed something to those that preceded it. As Raymond Moloney has pointed out, Zaïre was well placed to launch such an initiative.[36] Not only was Zaïre influenced by the Belgian liturgical movement before Vatican II, but Zaïrean musicians held ascendancy over the whole of sub-Saharan Africa, as leaders in musical taste and performance. The Zaïre Mass was the direct result of a decision by African bishops to take the conciliar and post-conciliar liturgical documents at their word and to exploit to the full the opportunities they offered. Raymond Moloney correctly judges that, while the Zaïre Mass does not 'break the mould of the Roman rite', it deserves to be called an inculturation, since it develops the principle of the vernacular and corresponds to a particular socio-cultural context.[37] In other words, the success of the Zaïre experiment relies less on the text, which was submitted to the scrutiny of the authorities for the best part of twenty years, than on the manner of celebration.

In December 1969, the Zaïrean bishops set in motion their project for a whole Eucharistic rite, not just a Eucharistic prayer, and faculties were granted for this by the Congregation for Divine Worship. Although, in 1971, the bishops accepted a text prepared by their Commission for Evangelization as a basis for experimentation, and an agreed version was published in 1975, its dissemination was accompanied by a proliferation of songs and musical settings in various languages, choreography, newly designed vestments and physical symbols.[38] This made the experimental Mass extremely popular, and, to some extent, relativized the process of securing textual approval. Nevertheless, negotiations began in 1983, and, after the text was formally ratified by the Zaïrean episcopal conference three years later, it was formally approved by the Congregation for Divine Worship on 30 April 1988.[39] This text is a slight restructuring of the Roman Order of Mass, according to an African anthropology of worship, and it contains numerous African themes, references and images, particularly in the Eucharistic prayer, which is a modification of the second of the four in the Roman Missal.[40]

In a culturally polycentric Church there would, however, be a need to create rites unforeseen by the Roman authorities and for which the Roman liturgical books provide no models. One of these is the practice of second burial, which takes place a year or so after death, and is familiar to anthropologists from the essay by Robert Hertz, the young Frenchman who died on active service in the First World War.[41] Although he based his theory on rituals practised by people in Indonesia, Malaysia and Borneo, as well as by the Aborigines of Australia and the Amerindians of North America, there are also plenty of corroborative examples from Africa. One of these is provided by the Shona people of Zimbabwe. According to Hertz, there are three aspects of the practice: rites which concern the physical remains of the dead person, the reinstatement of the deceased in a new mode of existence, and the final end of mourning by the bereaved. Unlike the Chagga of Tanzania in former times, or, indeed, the modern inhabitants of Madagascar, the Shona do not actually rebury the bones of the deceased, but they carry out a purification of the grave. They also reinstate the deceased within the family as an ancestral spirit through sacrificial offerings, and conclude the ceremonies with a ritual feast and dance.[42]

The Shona ceremony is known as *kurova guva*, 'smearing the grave', and its main purpose is to release the deceased from the land of isolation and bring him or her back to the family as an ancestral spirit who can be involved as guardian. The traditional ceremony involves divination, the use of anti-witchcraft medicines, the smearing of sacrificial beer on the grave and a graveside feast of roasted meat. Many of these elements were judged by missionaries to be incompatible with the Christian faith.

In time, *kurova guva* became something of a *cause célèbre*, and although the custom was opposed by Catholic missionaries from the outset, no headway could be made against it. Shona Catholics remained deeply attached to it. The bishops of Zimbabwe (then Rhodesia) appointed a commission in 1969 to study the rituals. After obtaining the general feeling of priests working among the Shona, by means of a questionnaire, the commission recommended that the ban on *kurova guva* be lifted on condition that certain erroneous beliefs and practices be corrected or abandoned.[43] The Zimbabwe bishops, for their part, preferred a functional substitution to the lifting of the ban, and they commissioned a Liturgy for Second Burial.[44] The bishops wanted a Catholic rite which was sufficiently close to the Shona original, so that people would feel that they had carried out their traditional obligations to the deceased and to the family. An experimental rite was issued in 1977 and a final liturgy closer to the Shona original in 1982.[45]

The ceremony may be performed with, or without, a priest

being present and consists of four stages: the preparation of the ritual grain for the beer, the offering of the beer, the presentation of the ritual animal, 'the goat of grief', and the homecoming of the spirit. The first stage is accompanied by prayer addressed to God and, conditionally, to the deceased, the grain being sprinkled with holy water, instead of traditional medicine. The beer offering is accompanied by a formula addressed to God on behalf of the deceased, and the immolation of the ritual animal is likened to the reconciliatory shedding of Christ's blood. Finally, the homecoming of the spirit and the rite of pouring beer and blood upon the grave make it clear that the deceased is being invited to join a heavenly, rather than an earthly, home.

While the creation of a Catholic *kurova guva* consists, up to a point, in textualizing an oral ritual, the formula for each stage is short and closely follows the style and spirit of the original. Most of the traditional ritual is retained, but given a Christian reinterpretation. A liturgy for second burial had not, of course, been foreseen by the liturgical books of the Roman rite, and the Zimbabwe bishops were free to be as creative as they wished. The constraints in this case came, not from Rome, but from local culture, if the Catholic liturgy was to be accepted as a credible substitute for the customary rites. The Zimbabwe Liturgy for Second Burial remains a *locus classicus* of African inculturation, the achievement of a sympathetic and courageous local hierarchy.

Another area of liturgical inculturation which presupposes local freedom and creativity is that of the liturgical homily. At the end of 1968, the author launched a homiletic experiment in which the Sunday homily took the form of an African (Kimbu) choric story, with a refrain to be sung at different points by the congregation.[46] A serious attempt was made to use Kimbu stories in these homilies, and while their original meaning was respected, it was amplified in the light of biblical teaching and Christian doctrine. An African, traditional theme was thus developed into a Christian theme; and it was felt that this was a way of identifying 'seeds of the Word' and of helping them to grow. Although the homilies were given in the Swahili language, they contained copious references to Kimbu language and literature.

The extraordinary enthusiasm which greeted this experiment exceeded all expectations, and news of the Kimbu homilies spread far beyond the villages in which they were preached. Some people appreciated the sung refrain and said that they found it difficult to listen to a monologue. Others liked the references to the Kimbu stories and customs, which made the message of the homily more real for them.

Since conducting this homiletic experiment in Ukimbu

129

(Tanzania) in 1968, I have continued to use the choric story format on many occasions when preaching in East Africa. Although this was a genuine case of independent invention, many African preachers naturally use the method. Cardinal Emmanuel Nsubuga, for example, (former) Archbishop of Kampala, Uganda, frequently gave the congregation the verse of a hymn to sing during a homily.[47] Within the constraints of its liturgical purpose, the homily is essentially a free composition of the preacher, who confers his own style upon it. A year after the Kimbu homiletic experiment, the Congregation for Divine Worship issued its instruction *Liturgiae Instaurationes*, which, among other things, speaks of the homily: 'The homily is the task of the priest: the faithful should refrain from comments, dialogue etc.'[48] This ruling was, no doubt, aimed at discussion, debate or even shared reflection taking the place of the traditional homily, rather than at the choric sermon.[49] Indeed, liturgists have revealed that the sung homily was an ancient Oriental practice of the fifth century. The *kontakion* was a metrical homily set to music, and rendered by a preacher–cantor, with the choir or congregation singing a refrain.[50] This could be regarded as a historical precedent for the choric sermon.

With regard to the cultural content of the homily, there have been several other initiatives involving the use of African oral literature. Declan Brosnan and Jon Kirby edited a collection of African parables which follow the cycles of the Roman Lectionary and provide thoughts for expounding the Sunday readings in the homily.[51] For some years, Donald Sybertz and Joseph Healey have been collecting Tanzanian proverbs, analysing and presenting them for homiletic and catechetical use.[52] The inculturation of the ministry of the Word is, beyond doubt, a developing reality in Africa.

If Africa – and indeed the rest of the world – is now familiar with the Roman rite, there is no sense in making an artificial break with the immediate Christian past. On the contrary, the new liturgies should grow organically from the old. As Eugene Uzukwu has suggested, special liturgical regions of the Roman rite should be created.[53] Within such regions, the local Churches would be able to create their own liturgical traditions and usages, without the meed to submit texts for central approval. Although appeal could be made to Rome in case of disputes and Rome could exercise a degree of supervision to safeguard authenticity, the basic initiative would belong to the local Church. Until such an arrangement comes into existence, the best hope for liturgical creativity – in Africa at least – lies with spontaneous, non-textual forms.

The exercise of the Petrine ministry in the new model of Church

The Pope is the successor of Peter in the college of bishops, who are themselves successors to the apostles. As such, he is the supreme pastor of the universal Church. He holds this office by virtue of his election to the Holy See of Rome, the final bishopric held by St Peter who, according to tradition, was also martyred there. Its co-founder was his fellow martyr St Paul, and the double apostolicity of its foundation adds to its prestige. When the Pope gives solemn blessings, solemn definitions or pronouncements, he does so in the name, and with the authority, of St Peter and St Paul. According to St Irenaeus, 'the faithful everywhere must needs agree with the Church at Rome'.[54] In virtue of this same bishopric, the Pope is also Patriarch of the West and Primate of Italy.

The history of the evolution of papal jurisdiction is well known. In the early Church most initiatives were taken by secular rulers, in particular episcopal appointments and the calling of councils. Gradually, Popes asserted their prerogatives, until – with the advent of the modern secular state – virtually all ecclesiastical powers pertaining to the Catholic Church were concentrated in papal hands. At the same time, the Roman Curia developed as the principal instrument of papal power. The College of Cardinals, which dates from the twelfth century, unites the more important pastoral archbishops of the world and leading curial officials as electors of the Pope, maintaining the fiction that they are the pastoral clergy – the suburbicarian bishops, the priests and deacons – of the city of Rome. Among the curial 'dicasteries' or departments of the Holy See, the Secretariat of State holds pride of place. It looks after the Church's general affairs and organizes the papal diplomatic service and the relations of the Holy See with national governments.

The Congregation for the Doctrine of the Faith, the former Holy Office, dates from the sixteenth century and safeguards the orthodoxy of Catholic doctrine and theology. The Congregation for the Oriental Churches regulates relations between the Holy See and the Catholic Oriental patriarchates. The Congregation for Divine Worship and Discipline of the Sacraments and the Congregation for the Causes of Saints need no explanation. The Congregation for Bishops deals with episcopal appointments worldwide. The Congregation for Evangelizing Peoples, the old Propaganda Fide, was founded in the seventeenth century to coordinate foreign missionary work throughout the world. Its prefect is popularly known as the 'Red Pope' and is thought to dispose of far greater material resources than the debt-stricken Vatican City itself. The Congregations for Clergy and for Institutes of Consecrated Life and Apostolic Life are self-explanatory, while the Congregation for Catholic Education co-ordinates the work of Catholic seminaries, universities and institutes of learning.

In addition to the congregations, there are numerous tribunals and pontifical councils, many of the latter having come into existence during or after the Second Vatican Council: Laity, Christian Unity, the Family, Justice and Peace, Migrants and Refugees, Inter-religious Dialogue, Non-Believers, Culture, Social Communications and so on. Impressive though this apparatus sounds, the Roman Curia is considerably smaller than the government and civil service of most countries. Moreover, there is an extensive sharing of personnel between its various departments.

The demands made on Pope and Curia by a greatly expanded and increasingly pluriform universal Church, with the greater part of its membership now in the southern hemisphere, threatens to make their offices almost unworkable. Pius XII hardly left the Vatican, but strove to speak knowledgeably to every specialized, professional constituency, an effort which was sometimes taken to absurd lengths, as when in 1947 he addressed the bee-keepers of Italy on the material, technical, psychological, biblical and liturgical interest of the bee.[55] John XXIII began a few tentative excursions from the Vatican to Italian shrines, but his great achievement was to have called a General Council of the Church. Paul VI chose symbolic destinations for his journeys, the Holy Land, the United Nations, Bombay, Medellín, Kampala and so on. John Paul II's pastoral journeys have taken him to every corner of Italy and the world, sometimes more than once to the same place. The astonishing litany of languages heard in St Peter's Square every Easter Sunday morning is a papal *tour de force*, but one which, like the papal journeys, risks becoming invidious as the list grows longer.

No doubt every Pope is free to develop his own style, but the papal office is becoming one for which it is increasingly difficult to find a candidate. The untimely death of John Paul I underlines this point. Moreover, it appears that the populist, ultramontane papacy is becoming more and more extended, until perhaps an eventual breaking-point may be reached. Pope John Paul II's zeal in conducting worldwide pastoral journeys is admirable in itself, but such journeys cannot be a substitute for a culturally polycentric Church. It is inconceivable for one individual, however exalted his office, to identify credibly with so many cultures and contexts, let alone to do so exhaustively and impartially. Inevitably it must run the risk of becoming an alienation or a sham.

Some writers have suggested that the papacy should revert to the more passive role which it exercised in the early Church, and that the Pope should concentrate on his own diocese of Rome, waiting merely to be called on by the other local Churches for arbitration or guidance. Personally, I do not believe that the Petrine ministry should be exercised in this way. One cannot make abstraction of the historical development of Church and papacy. Moreover, the Petrine ministry within, and towards, the universal Church should be an active, not a passive, ministry. It should be a genuine service to Catholicity, exercised conjointly with the local episcopates, and as head of the whole episcopal college.

It is not suggested that there should be any change or modification of the Pope's power, but that it should be exercised in the context of the new Church model. Echoing another famous passage from St Irenaeus, the Second Vatican Council's Dogmatic Constitution on the Church spoke of the relationship between the Pope and local Churches, as follows:

> Holding a rightful place in the communion of the Church there are also particular Churches that retain their own traditions, without prejudice to the Chair of Peter which presides over the whole assembly of charity, and protects their legitimate variety while at the same time taking care that these differences do not hinder unity, but rather contribute to it.[56]

What is at issue in the new model is not the Pope's role of protecting existing legitimate differences in the Church, but of actually legitimizing new differences. Such legitimization must be far-reaching and widespread. In other words, the Pope's service to Catholicity must be characteristically embodied in the sanctioning of cultural pluriformity. There should be no imposition of a single, Roman outlook, or of a narrow Roman theology. Above all, there should be no fear of ideas which arise in other local Churches to challenge the Roman outlook. The Roman Curia must listen in order to learn, not simply in order to condemn. Moreover, it should be prepared to acknowledge its own internal pluriformity. Rome speaks with many voices. Not only are there variations of emphasis between curial departments, but Popes, like other world leaders, have speech-writers and researchers who reflect differing views, otherwise it would be impossible to account for the contradictions within and between papal or curial documents. It would be reassuring to know the provenance of the many documents that are issued under the signature, or in the name, of the Pope, and to learn who is hiding behind the throne.

Whether or not the curial departments should remain as they are (and there does seem to be a case for scaling them down), the one thing to which they should all be dedicated is safeguarding and legitimizing the differences among local Churches, as well as the bond of faith and order that unites them. The Vatican should have four main functions: confirming the faith of the local Churches, offering leadership and guidance to them through their bishops, operating a mechanism of mutual enrichment between them, and providing them with a resource centre for this.

The faith is confirmed when the orthodoxy and orthopraxis of the local Churches is upheld. This should be done as far as possible by prophetic gestures, rather than by more and more written texts. Such gestures have far greater value for evangelization, as the papal pastoral journeys have shown. The Pope, as shepherd and teacher of all Christians, should address them, as far as possible, through the voice of their own bishops. During the Second Vatican Council, Pope Paul VI was reluctant to impose himself on the Council Fathers. He set the agenda of the Council. He floated his ideas in the *aula* through other speakers, and dialogued with his brother bishops as the debates took place. Occasionally, he took his place among the Council presidents. After the Council, it was left to him to establish the norms by which the bishops' decisions would be applied. I believe that this is an excellent model of how Popes should relate to the episcopal college, tactfully, sensitively, offering inspiration, encouragement, at times – when necessary – confrontation.

Mutual enrichment or invigoration was the keynote of Paul VI's vision of world-Church communion.[57] We have already discussed the concept of a cross-cultural hermeneutic and the need for a central mechanism of exchange in ideas, as well as in mutual ministry or mission. The Petrine role is not to impose a single theology or a single expression of the one faith, but to safeguard the faith by encouraging a listening process among those who represent the varied expressions of faith. A resource centre that is truly universal in its pluriformity needs to be set up, so that information and experience can be exchanged in all the recognized fields of evangelization and inculturation: theology, catechesis, liturgy, law, religious life, ecclesial structures and ministries. The emphasis should be placed on mutual service and mutual empowering, not on centralized approval or disapproval. As far as possible, policy decisions should be taken by the local Churches themselves, since that is where evangelization actually takes place.

There is no doubt that this requires a totally different mindset from the one prevailing at present in the Roman Curia. It demands a practical acknowledgement that the Holy Spirit is at work in and among the local Churches, and on the frontiers of the Church universal. It calls for a recognition that local Churches already influence one another. It requires a readiness to listen to, and learn from, others – the very antithesis of current attitudes, according to which all that is done elsewhere in the Church must be deduced from principles enunciated in Rome. St Irenaeus exhorted other Churches to 'agree with the Church at Rome'. This does not mean that agreement is a one-way process; far from it. Indeed, St Irenaeus was at pains to demonstrate that this agreement of faith concerned 'the meaning of the tradition', and that it united Christians of many different languages and backgrounds.[58]

Finally, episcopal appointments must respect a truly emergent leadership. There is nothing so harmful to effective evangelization as the appointment of leaders who do not enjoy the confidence and respect of those they are supposed to lead. This means that consultation must be genuine. If religious are entitled to elect their superiors, and cardinals to elect the Pope, why should it not also be possible for ordinary priests and laity to elect their bishop? At any rate, a new bishop should be a gift and not a threat to his diocese.

In the next chapter, we shall look at the new model of Church from another angle – from that of the grass roots. If the local Church is the primary ecclesial reality, and the actual theatre or field of evangelization itself, then the shape of this local Church must conform to the needs of evangelization. As we shall see, however much it needs to be organized or serviced from the centre, evangelization emerges ultimately from below, and is the work of grass roots communities.

References

1 *Lumen Gentium*, 48–51.
2 Karl Rahner, *Theological Investigations*, vol. 6 (London: Darton, Longman and Todd, 1974), pp. 253–94.
3 Cf. John XXIII and the future Paul VI, quoted in Peter Hebblethwaite, *John XXIII – Pope of the Council* (London: Geoffrey Chapman, 1984), p. 109.
4 *Lumen Gentium*, 22.
5 *Justice in the World* (Boston: St Paul Editions, November 1971), p. 15.
6 *Christus Dominus*, 27; *Ecclesiae Sanctae*, 16 (2).
7 *Redemptoris Missio*, 42.
8 Edward Schillebeeckx, *Interim Report on the Books 'Jesus' and 'Christ'* (London: SCM Press, 1980), p. 54.

9 Cf. Aylward Shorter, *Revelation and Its Interpretation* (London: Geoffrey Chapman, 1983), pp. 111–13.

10 Bernard Lonergan, *Method in Theology* (London: Darton, Longman and Todd, 1975), p. 276. My parentheses.

11 Cf. *Evangelii Nuntiandi*, 63, for the concept of mutual 'enrichment'.

12 Peter Hebblethwaite, 'The Bishops' Part', *The Tablet* (5 May 1993), pp. 609–10.

13 *L'Osservatore Romano* (28 June 1982), pp. 1–8.

14 This was the point of view of Pedro Arrupe at the 1977 Synod of Bishops. Cf. *African Ecclesial Review*, vol. 20, no. 1 (1978), pp. 32–3.

15 J. B. Metz, 'Unity and Diversity: Problems and Prospects for Inculturation', *Concilium*, no. 204 (1989), p. 85.

16 Ibid.; Michel Legrain, 'Young Churches and the New Code of Canon Law', *Theology Digest*, vol. 31 (1984) pp. 217–18; John M. Huels, 'Interpreting Canon Law in Diverse Cultures', *The Jurist*, vol. 47 (1987), pp. 249–93.

17 *Ad Gentes Divinitus*, 19; *Ecclesiae Sanctae* III, 19 (2).

18 Legrain, op. cit., pp. 217–18.

19 *Acts of the Fifth Plenary Assembly of the Symposium of Episcopal Conferences of Africa and Madagascar* (Nairobi, 1978), p. 225.

20 Cf. 'Report on the Church in Africa', no. 6, in R. Hickey (ed.), *Modern Missionary Documents and Africa* (Dublin: Dominican Publications, 1982), pp. 241–2.

21 Aylward Shorter, 'Something New for Africa', *The Tablet* (22 September 1990), pp. 1208–9; Aylward Shorter, *The African Synod – A Personal Response to the Outline Document* (Nairobi: St Paul Publications – Africa, 1991), pp. 9–28.

22 Aylward Shorter, 'Cooked in a Roman Pot', *The Tablet* (3 April 1993), pp. 446–7.

23 Bede the Venerable, *A History of the English Church and People* (Harmondsworth: Penguin Books, 1955), I, 30.

24 S. C. de Propaganda Fide, *Collectanea* (Rome, 1907), cap x, no. 300, p. 103.

25 Cf. *Notitiae*, 44 (1969), p. 12.

26 *Sacrosanctum Concilium*, 35.

27 Aidan Kavanagh, 'Liturgy' in Adrian Hastings (ed.), *Modern Catholicism* (London: SPCK, 1991), p. 71.

28 Anscar J. Chupungco, *Liturgical Inculturation, Sacramentals, Religiosity and Catechesis* (Collegeville, Minnesota: Liturgical Press, 1992), p.51.

29 *Orientalium Ecclesiarum*, 2.

30 Hickey, op. cit., p. 203.

31 Boniface Luykx, *Culte Chrétien en Afrique après Vatican II* (Immensee, Switzerland: *Neue Zeitschrift für Missionswissenschaft*, 22, 1974).

32 The author assisted at the Ndzon Melen Mass, in Yaoundé, on Sunday 3 December 1972.

33 Aylward Shorter, 'An African Eucharistic Prayer', *African Ecclesial Review*, vol. 12, no. 2 (1970), pp. 143–8; Aylward Shorter, *African Culture and the Christian Church* (London: Geoffrey Chapman, 1973/Maryknoll, NY: Orbis Books, 1974), pp. 114–16 (for a more complete revised version); Aylward Shorter, 'Prière Eucharistique Africaine', trans. P. Kooy and L. Kuntz,

Bulletin des Missions Africaines de Lyon, vol. 7, no. 4 (1970); also in *Spiritus*, no. 52 (1973), pp. 109–11.

34 Cf. Eugene E. Uzukwu, 'All-Africa Eucharistic Prayer: A Critique', *African Ecclesial Review*, vol. 21, no. 5 (1979), pp. 338–47; and *Liturgy: Truly Christian, Truly African* (Spearhead 74) (Gaba 1982).

35 Eugene E. Uzukwu, 'Blessing and Thanksgiving among the Igbo: Towards an African Eucharistic Prayer', *African Ecclesial Review*, vol. 22, no. 1 (1980), pp. 17–22.

36 Raymond Moloney, 'The Zaïrean Mass and Inculturation', *Worship*, vol. 62, no. 5 (1988), pp. 433–42.

37 Moloney, ibid., pp. 440–1.

38 'The Zaïre Rite for the Mass', *African Ecclesial Review*, vol. 17, no. 4 (1975), pp. 243–8.

39 Jean Evénou, 'Le Missel Romain pour les Diocèses du Zaïre', *Notitiae 264*, vol. 24, no. 7 (1988), pp. 454–72.

40 Moloney, op. cit., pp. 434–5.

41 Robert Hertz, *Death and the Right Hand* (London: Cohen and West, 1960), pp. 53–76.

42 Zimbabwe Episcopal Conference, '*Kurova Guva* Ceremony and Christianity' (mimeographed report, Harare, 1978); Michael Gelfand, *Shona Religions* (Cape Town, 1962), pp. 129, 134–5.

43 'Report of the Commission Appointed to Investigate the Kurova Guva Ceremony' (typescript in the author's possession, no date); Charles Mafurutu, 'Kurova Guva Ceremony' (manuscript in the author's possession, 1970).

44 For the notion of functional substitution, cf. Gerald A. Arbuckle, *Earthing the Gospel* (London: Geoffrey Chapman/Maryknoll, NY: Orbis Books, 1990), pp. 10–11.

45 Zimbabwe Catholic Bishops' Conference, 'Liturgy for the Second Burial' (mimeographed translation from Shona, 1982).

46 Aylward Shorter, 'Form and Content in the African Sermon: An Experiment', *African Ecclesial Review*, vol. 11, no. 3 (1969), pp. 265–79; Aylward Shorter, *Priest in the Village* (London: Geoffrey Chapman, 1979), pp. 173–9.

47 The author witnessed this on several occasions during his eight-year stay in Uganda.

48 *Liturgiae Instaurationes*, 2 (a): Austin Flannery (ed.), *Documents on Vatican Council II* (Dublin: Dominican Publications, 1975).

49 Cf. William J. Byron, 'The Dialogue Homily: A Practice in Search of a Theory', *Worship*, vol. 44, no. 2 (1970), pp. 112–16.

50 R. J. Schork, 'Sung Sermon', *Worship*, vol. 47, no. 9 (1973), pp. 527–39.

51 Declan Brosnan and Jon Kirby, *African Parables: Thoughts for Sunday Readings* (Occasional Papers of Tamale Institute of Cross-Cultural Studies 1 and 2; Tamale, Ghana, 1988).

52 Donald Sybertz and Joseph Healey, *Kueneza Injili Kwa Methali* ('Spreading the Gospel through Proverbs') (Ndanda-Peramiho, 1984).

53 Eugene Uzukwu, 'Food and Drink in Africa: The Christian Eucharist', *African Ecclesial Review*, vol. 22, no. 6 (1980), p. 383.

54 Irenaeus, *Adversus Haereses*, III; cf. Henry Bettenson, *The Early Christian Fathers* (Oxford: Oxford University Press, 1956), p. 122.

55 Cf. Pontifical Court Club, London, *Catholic Documents*, vol. 1, p. 1 (27 November 1947).
56 *Lumen Gentium*, 13; Irenaeus, *Adversus Haereses*, III, 16, 6; III, 22, 1–3.
57 *Evangelii Nuntiandi*, 62–63.
58 Irenaeus, *Adversus Haereses*, I, x, 1–2; cf. Bettenson, op. cit., p. 127.

6 Evangelization from below

God comes to us from below

In 1977 Andrew Hake coined the phrase 'urbanization from below'. He was referring to the social process in the urban squatter areas of African cities.[1] In 1988 I applied his idea to the evangelization of culture and spoke of 'inculturation from below'.[2] The point I was making was that genuine inculturation cannot come from above. It must originate with the local community. We are all probably familiar with the idea of 'Christology from below', of beginning a theology of Christ with the man Jesus and his own developing understanding of his divine identity and mission. It is an approach which brings Jesus closer to us and enables us to know God through his human face. In point of fact, God has revealed himself from below, by dwelling amongst us. Theologians of liberation like to speak of 'history from below', or 'the underside of history'. The fact is that revelation and salvation come from below – or, at least, via the below.

We can apply the idea of movement 'from below' to the whole of evangelization. Evangelization originates in the Christian community from which the evangelizers themselves emerge, and from the experience of Jesus in the community who sends them from its midst. When we reach this understanding, we realize at once that this is the key to successful evangelization. Moreover, we are developing still further the argument of the last chapter in this book – the argument for a new model of Church, a model that pays greater attention to the Church of the grass roots, and that guarantees a more effective evangelization.

A few years ago, when I was attached to the staff of a large Nairobi slum parish, I met a young man called John Musyoka.[3] John was in his early twenties, a university student, intelligent and good-looking, but deprived of his eyesight since birth. He had attended a school for the blind run by the Salvation Army. The

Salvationists had taught him to read and write in Braille and had prepared him for university entrance. At their school, he had become a Christian, embracing an evangelical faith, in which he proclaimed Jesus Christ as his personal Saviour.

At the university he encountered Catholics from our parish and eventually became critical of the Christian individualism that he recognized in himself. His friends introduced him to the basic Christian communities of the parish, to their communal prayer, celebrations and Bible study, as well as to their collective action for welfare and social justice in the squatter area. He was immediately attracted, he told me, by this communitarian Christianity and asked to be received into the Catholic Church.

Sponsored by his basic community, he joined the catechumenate. The programme lasted a full year and he attended the classes and meetings with regularity and enthusiasm. Once or twice in term-time I drove him back to the university, and he shared his new-found faith with me on the way. All the liturgical steps in the Rite of Christian Initiation for Adults were taken, with his basic community playing it full part in vouching for him and introducing him to active Catholic life. Finally, I had the joy of baptizing him during the Easter Vigil which concluded his catechumenate.

No doubt there are dangers of externalism and manipulation in such catechumenate programmes, but where there is a genuine experience of Christian community, they exemplify the best characteristics of evangelization from below. Members of the community are the evangelizers and they offer the evangelized a share in their community life. Moreover, they accompany the candidate, sponsor him or her and celebrate every step of the pilgrimage towards full membership of the Church. In this case, no doubt, John's personal faith and social conscience, acquired from the Salvation Army, were fulfilled and enlarged by the Catholic community dimension.

It is also worth underlining the role which the liturgy plays in the process of conversion. Not only is the conversion process spelt out, as it were, in liturgical fashion, with symbolic actions expressing the candidate's growing commitment, but adhesion to a Christian community is often sparked off in the very first place by a liturgical experience. Liturgy is the public prayer of the local Christian community – the community at prayer. John Musyoka, like many Catholic converts, found that liturgical celebration was a revelation. Many such people, especially those exposed to prejudice or discriminatory teaching, take part in the Mass out of curiosity. They then discover that their prejudice is unfounded and that the Eucharistic liturgy makes a quite different impression upon them. Many are immediately fascinated by it, and are certain of God's presence in the celebration.

Evangelization works through ordinary relationships and ordinary experiences. It comes from below. For this reason the sociology of conversion is an important subject of study for those aiming at a more effective evangelization. God works through the ordinary processes and structures of human society, and expects evangelizers to use their reason in working out a strategy that accords with social realities. Potentially receptive audiences need to be targeted, as was pointed out in Chapter 1. Once again, we are in the realm of 'the below', dealing with socio-cultural motivations and determinants. These do not detract from the truth of the Gospel, but they do channel its message and frequently they prevent people from recognizing its truth. At its most extreme, such social analysis can become a calculated strategy of Church growth, but two things need to be borne in mind. One is that, apart from the fact that a human society's response to the Gospel may be extremely complex, God's revelation/salvation is not, in fact, solely determined by human calculation and effort. The other is that the evangelizer still has a duty towards the normally unreceptive elements of society and can count on the activity of the Holy Spirit to address them.

More than twenty years ago, Louise Pirouet, a historian of the African Church, made a comparative study of responses to the Gospel in three East African societies.[4] In the Kingdom of Toro, in Uganda, Anglican missionaries made a bid to set up an established Church on the English pattern. Their interest in converting the Omukama and his court coincided with the latter's need of Church support for the institutions of kingship under the colonial regime. There was no real conflict of interest between Christianity and Toro culture. The danger consisted in the Church becoming identified with a traditional regime that was swept away at independence. As these words are being written, Uganda is set to restore the Kingdom of Toro, but it is unlikely that the Anglican Church will allow itself to be so closely involved again.

The Iteso, in eastern Uganda, were very far from being organized into a centralized kingdom. They were settled pastoralists with a stratified age-set system. Moreover the Church got off on the wrong foot, as it were, with the Iteso, by approaching them through an interloping Ganda chieftain who was already a Christian. The missionaries were also guilty of condescension towards the Iteso, whom they considered outlandish, and they came with the explicit intention of 'civilizing' them, founding schools and introducing cotton as a cash crop. They did little, however, to root the Christian faith deeply in the Teso culture. They were too busy

141

'civilizing' the Iteso to come to understand their way of life. As a result the Iteso never became sufficiently interested in Christianity, although they welcomed the educational and development opportunities brought by the missionaries.

A complete contrast, however, was provided by the evangelization of the Kikuyu of central Kenya. Here the missionaries made a frontal attack on the indigenous culture, especially on the traditional practice of female circumcision, which they understandably regarded as barbaric. Missionaries, therefore, challenged the Kikuyu way of life at a crucial point – the initiation ceremonies – and Kikuyu Christians were obliged to renounce this practice on conversion. This was a heavy price to pay for their new faith and it was further tested by the nationalist Mau Mau campaign, which violently attacked those who rejected traditional culture. As a result the Kikuyu Church became stronger, rather than weaker, and, when Mau Mau was over, there was a wave of mass conversions. The Catholic Church, in particular, which had been more accommodating towards the initiation rites, but which had condemned the savagery of Mau Mau, was seen as offering a means of reconciliation. The Kikuyu Church is vigorous today because of a moment of crisis in which Christianity was present and seen to be culturally and morally relevant.

These examples adduced by Louise Pirouet show how complex is a society's response to the Gospel. Another factor which is certainly relevant in the case of missionary evangelization is the culture of the missionaries themselves and the cultural form of their own Christian faith and practice. Missionaries came to nineteenth-century Africa from unitary European states in which the Church often occupied a privileged position. Their own Christian history began with the making of key converts, King Ethelbert of Kent or King Clovis of the Franks, or with the crowning of a Christian leader like the Emperor Charlemagne. It was understandable, therefore, that the missionaries were attracted by unitary African kingdoms and they should have directed their attention to the royal circles and the ruling classes. Christian evangelization in Africa registered its greatest successes in Uganda, Rwanda, Burundi, northern Tanzania and Lesotho, all places where there were unitary traditional rulers and kingdoms. Nomadic, stratified and nucleated societies, like those of the East African pastoralists and the Nilotic peoples, were neglected. Missionaries could not discover how to gear their understanding of a territorially based Christianity to such unfamiliar polities and alien social environments. As a result, these ethnic groups have been the very last to be effectively evangelized, and in some cases evangelization has had to wait upon socio-cultural change triggered by secular processes.

By the beginning of the third millennium roughly half the world's population will be urban-dwelling. Even in Africa half the continent's population will be urban-dwelling by the first quarter of the next century. The influx of urban migrants into the low income areas of Third World cities is too fast for an often rurally biased Church to catch up with.[5] Evangelization in the city is an urgent necessity if the Church is to survive in the modern age, but it demands a different strategy from evangelization in the rural areas. The Church has to offer urban centres of integration, stability and prayer which attract the migrants. It cannot impose a rigid, territorial, parish structure on the town. This also illustrates the need for an evangelization from below, a movement that takes into account the realities of urban social and cultural life.

Evangelization and basic communities

Evangelization is most effective when it operates through interpersonal relationships. These relationships are to be found ideally in the family, through the mutual influence of marriage partners or of parents and children. In Nairobi archdiocese (Kenya) a pool of young evangelizers has recently been set up, and meetings are arranged between these young people and members of the parental generation, so that they can witness their faith and discover ways of communicating with each other. The influence of peer groups is often stronger than that of the family, and young people are more powerfully impressed by them. This explains the influence of Christian student and young professional movements. Role models also enter into the picture: teachers, stars of screen, stage and stadium, and – when present – the Christian sentiments of a popular song repertoire.

Urban social organization is characterized more by interpersonal or 'ego-centred' networks than by communities and groups. This is because urban life is focused on the workplace, rather than on the place of residence. Individuals live near their work, often in suburban housing estates, and create their own selective neighbourhood. In such a situation good neighbourliness is an important form of interpersonal relationship. The charity and concern of the Christian neighbour can be one of the most successful forms of evangelization. Christians are commanded by Christ to be neighbours to those in need. 'Go and do the same', he told the lawyer, at the end of the parable about the Good Samaritan (Luke 10:25–37). We are to love our neighbours, which means showing them the love of a neighbour, since neighbourliness denotes the relationship of two people paired in a single role. Evangelization is a direct fulfilment of the great commandment of love directed towards God and neighbour, and good neighbourliness is its expression. The Christian community encourages and practises good neighbourliness in its care for those in need, and in its practical pursuit of justice and peace. The caring Church is a Church engaged in evangelization.

In spite of all that has just been said, community remains a privileged form of interpersonal relationship, and this in practice means some form of basic community. The sense of community can be more or less intense depending on the social situation. It has already been pointed out that networks are more characteristic of urban and suburban living than communities. While this is true, it is also the case that there is a greater measure of solidarity among the urban poor, which favours community-building. There are even elements for community-building in suburbia, which I believe can be developed into basic communities. As we saw in Chapter 3, these are chiefly issue-centred groups which could be harnessed to the parish pastoral ministry.

The basic Christian community is essentially a cell of committed Christians at the service of the Church and of the world. It is a group that draws fullness of life from Word and Sacrament in the midst of human realities – the joys and consolations of daily life, but particularly the experience of oppression, suffering, sickness and death. The Word of God, read, reflected upon and celebrated in community, provides answers to such vital questions. Together, the members seek to apply God's Word to their own lives and actually to live it in their community context. This is essentially the work of evangelization. It comprises all the integral elements of evangelization: inculturation, liberation and dialogue.

The *Instrumentum Laboris*, or working document of the Special Assembly of the Synod of Bishops for Africa, has recognized the intimate connection between inculturation and the life of basic Christian communities. In probably its most eloquent passage on inculturation we find the following:

> Those responsible in pastoral matters should analyse the nature of inculturation of Christianity in Africa and its capacity to constitute vibrant ecclesial communities, the role of the laity, the response to the thirst for spiritual experience and the Word of God, as well as the reply to be given to the vital questions posed by suffering, sickness and death.[6]

The basic Christian community is concerned first and foremost with the problem of how to be a Christian in a given life context.

Its task is to penetrate the local culture and bring the values of the Gospel to bear upon it, as well as to discover authentic ways of living the same Gospel in accordance with the traditional outlooks and forms of expression of this culture. It seeks new ways of living, speaking and celebrating the Christian faith, ways which are appropriate to the specific life context of the basic community. In a word, the basic Christian community is evangelizing the local culture, as well as those who adhere to this culture.

Inculturation, as we have seen, is intimately connected with dialogue. It presupposes an ongoing dialogue with human cultures, traditions and religions. At a popular level, basic Christian communities are engaged in such dialogue. Their members rub shoulders with people of other Churches and other faiths. They regularly encounter cultures and religions which oblige them to carry out a discernment to discover what is of God – or indeed of Christ – in them. They approach these other traditions in a spirit of love, of optimism and generosity, not of suspicion, hostility or prejudice. They carry out joint action for social justice with them. In the Western world they encounter a secularized, technological culture which requires an even more subtle discernment, because it so closely affects the lives of the community members themselves. The basic Christian community strives to rekindle the flame of faith in the neighbourhood and to restore the awareness of God's presence in society.

Finally, the basic Christian community is engaged in liberation. It lives the Gospel by sponsoring development projects of its own, where this is possible. It carries out social analysis, identifying the proximate and remote causes of social problems. It tries to make its own small contribution to the solution of these problems, correcting abuses of human rights and resisting oppression. It is committed to human promotion in all its forms. Even more staunchly, it is committed to the restoration of social morality and the liberation from personal, as well as social, sin. As Pope John Paul II pointed out in *Redemptoris Missio*, true faith demands a free adherence on the part of human beings and is essentially directed towards human freedom.[7] The basic Christian community is an instrument of this liberation, serving the personal dignity and responsibility of humanity by hearing, proclaiming, celebrating and living the Word of God and the Good News of his Kingdom.

Basic Christian communities also enjoy a structural freedom which is one of their most advantageous assets in evangelization. They are not simply an appendage of the Church's hierarchy, nor are they by definition a segment of the Church's territorial structure. They do not feature, for example, in the Church's Code of Canon Law. Of course, it goes without saying that they operate within the Church's structure of parish, deanery and diocese, and are subject to hierarchical authority. It is also a necessary condition that they be ecclesial, that is to say, that they are a genuine instance of Church, and also agents in the pastoral self-care of the parish, co-operating directly with the pastoral team. Nevertheless, this does not make them a structural part of the parish, still less adjuncts of the priestly ministry itself. On the contrary, basic Christian communities are free-floating groups of Christians who have freely joined together. They exist wherever there are committed Christians and committed Christian leaders, ready to come together and to place themselves at the disposal of their pastors. They cannot be coerced any more than a couple should be coerced to get married. They are not mere reporters or deputies of a parish neighbourhood or of a parish council ward. They have a life of their own. Like all genuine communities, the achievement of community itself is their first goal. It is for this reason that basic Christian community-building is not just a process of dividing up the parish map and telling Christians to form themselves into communities. On the contrary, it is a search for committed leaders and followers, wherever they are situated in the parish.

A 'basic communities Church' is a Church in which basic Christian communities are found at the grass roots in every parish. What makes this kind of Church so exciting is that it is opposed to a totalitarian model of Church. It is a model in which the tail can really wag the dog as it were – in other words, initiatives can really come from below. Moreover, its evangelization is effective for the reason that the apostolate of the laity is effective, namely because it is inserted in the actual life context of Christians, plus the fact that it is an instrument of the pastoral team. Structurally, the basic Christian community enjoys the benefits of both verticality and horizontality.

Evangelization and collaborative ministry

We are all familiar with the idea of a parish catechist, male or female, operating under the direct authority of the parish priest. However, evangelization can be made more effective through team ministry, and especially through collaborative ministry. Team ministry denotes a situation in which the various parish ministries are brought together with the pastors in a single team, thereby multiplying the effort of one or two clergy. Religious sisters, catechists, youth leaders, Eucharistic ministers, readers, social workers work together with their priests as a team, shaping the policy of the parish, fulfilling its perceived goals and giving expression to the proclamation and implementation of the Word of God.

Collaborative ministry means bringing together different conditions and classes of people in order to make evangelization more effective. In the first place this means the collaboration of the sexes. In the basic Christian community this collaboration can be realized in a manner that is not, at the moment, possible at other levels of the Church. Instead of women being subordinated to an all-male clergy, they can work together with men on a footing of equality, and can even assume positions of leadership. The collaboration of men and women in the evangelizing tasks of the basic Christian community offers a more powerful witness and is generally more efficient in making contact with different categories of people. Collaborative ministry has nothing to do with a power-struggle between the sexes for leadership in the Church. It has nothing ostensibly to do with human rights, or even theological reasoning. Its value lies in making the Church's work of evangelization more effective. If the Church really wishes to evangelize more successfully, then it must give an ever greater welcome to collaborative ministry.

Here again, the basic Christian community may be carrying out a prophetic role towards the Church at large. The success of evangelization from below, of a basic communities Church, may prepare a mentality which is more favourable towards giving women a place in the leadership of the Roman Catholic Church and towards keeping open the question of women's ordination. The free-floating character of the basic Christian community gives it greater freedom, more spontaneity and a dynamism that is lacking in the Church's official structures and ministries. Above all it can reflect more visibly the actual constitution of humanity and the evangelizing Church. Members of basic Christian communities, men and women, carry out a real ministry of revelation/salvation to those around them. In many cases, they also exercise lay ministries at parish level. They are also engaged in programmes of parish renewal and in the pastoral planning conducted by the parish pastoral team.

Collaboration, however, is not just partnership between the sexes. It includes other categories. Chief among these is that of the youth. Through basic communities, as well as through specialized youth groups, the potential of young people for evangelization can also be realized. This is important in any community, but it is vital in countries, like many in the non-Western world, where young people make up the majority of the whole population, and where they are traditionally subordinated to older generations in both public and private affairs. It is essential that new roles be created for the growing numbers of young people, and that they should have their own ministry within the parish. The basic Christian community can be an instrument for the emergent youth to take its responsibilities with regard to evangelization.

Basic Christian communities cut across many other human barriers, visible and invisible. Such barriers include those of age, race, ethnic group, language, educational background and class. In many parishes, there is a strong temptation for Christians to come together on an ethnic or language basis, or on the basis of some other common interest. This is not in itself wrong. However, the logic of the great commandment and of the great commission demands that such barriers should also be overridden. This was the striking lesson of Pentecost itself, when language barriers were overcome and everyone heard the marvels of God and proclaimed them together in a new language of love (Acts 2:1–40). 'And many believed the message and were baptized.' Nothing could be more effective for evangelization than this demonstration of solidarity. Moreover, the life witness of such a group is equally compelling, since it reaches into so many different areas of experience.

The basic Christian community can therefore be a privileged instance of collaboration in the Church's work of evangelization. It can exemplify the very meaning of Catholicity and the way in which the Church serves the spread of God's Kingdom. The basic Christian community provides an apt instrument – and an ecclesial instrument – for the Holy Spirit to use in God's loving dialogue with the world, making his Word known and offering his salvation to humanity. The essential collaboration, therefore, is that between the basic Christian community and the Spirit at work in the world. This is the humble and joyful service of God's people – the loving mutuality which makes Christianity attractive and credible. It is the witness which confers meaning and purpose on life. It offers an experience which transforms people, which gives a voice to the silent, which emboldens women to speak up for their interests and concerns in front of the whole community, and which enables young people also to take on new roles of witness and service.

Through this collaborative dimension, the basic Christian community makes a vital contribution to the development of the whole Church, and makes it a more effective instrument of evangelization. If the Church should ever turn its back on the relatively recent experience of basic Christian communities or should hinder their spread to the rest of the world, it would do so at the expense of its commitment to evangelization.

Renewal from below

The outsider view of the Roman Catholic Church is often that of a highly authoritarian body, arrogantly exercising total control over the minds, consciences and mores of its members. Its dogmatic teaching is often thought to be naively uncompromising, its moral demands intransigent and mostly concerned with sex. It is believed to brook no opposition, and to exercise to the full its power to excommunicate, condemn and dismiss every kind of dissident. The charism of infallibility – it is often believed by the outsider – offers Church authority an excuse for acting in a dictatorial and capricious manner, without the need for informing its own conscience before coercing the consciences of others. Generally, this caricature is condemned by the press and other mass media – but not because it is a caricature. A few outsiders, however, profess to marvel at the strong moral leadership which it purports to give. Others take the caricature for an unrealized ideal and contrast it with the results of opinion polls showing the extent to which ordinary Catholics manage to evade this adamantine authority and to ignore its teachings.

In Chapter 5 we examined factors which may be the cause of such a caricature. However, it does remain a caricature. The misfortune is that, in order to understand the Roman Catholic Church, the press and other media focus all their attention on the Vatican and on the papal *magisterium*. No doubt, the Petrine ministry, however it is carried out, is an indispensable component of Roman Catholicism, and a powerful force for good in the world. No doubt also, communion with the Roman Church is believed by Catholics to be necessary in order to belong to the universal Church, but it is not the Church's primary reality. That quality is given by the Second Vatican Council to the local or particular Church in communion with Rome.[8] The universal Church is made up of local Churches, and it is these which represent the Church's everyday face. This face is a human face, and the Church should be recognized by it.

What is this human face? The local Church, and particularly one which is communities-based, presents a Church that is in touch with real life situations. It is primarily a worshipping church, intimately and faithfully celebrating the mysteries of Christ in the liturgy, especially in the Eucharist. It is a Bible-reading Church, in which Christians seek guidance for their lives in Holy Scripture. It is a caring Church, one that shows continuous compassion for the poor and disadvantaged. It is a 'solidarity' Church in which pastoral ministry is shared, under the leadership of the priest. Its authority, like that of Jesus Christ, imposes itself because of its consistency, sincerity and quiet certainty. It is very far from being a 'fascist' Church which orders, threatens and punishes. On the contrary, its ideal is one of relentless, loving service.

The communities-based local Church is not arrogant. On the contrary, its chief mark is humility. It is humble enough to know the limits of dogmatic formulations. It knows how to relativize rules and regulations and how to discern a hierarchy among truths. It humbly offers its service of evangelization to the Holy Spirit at work in the world, for the building of God's Kingdom. It is not a self-serving Church, but a selfless one. It realizes the necessity of being in the world, but not of it. Its preoccupations are with justice, love and life. It reaches out to other local Churches, to other Christian communions, to other faith traditions. But above all, it is focused on Jesus Christ, quietly confident of being on the right track – with him. In a word, it is an optimistic Church, really believing in the ultimate victory of Christ over evil.

Such is – or should be – the portrait of the Church emerging from below, the portrait of the evangelizing Church. Would that the world's media would pay more attention to it! In the Catholic Church initiatives for renewal do not normally come from above. After all, those who exercise authority have a vested interest in maintaining the *status quo*. But renewal really does begin at the grass roots, even though it takes time to win acceptance at the higher levels. The Church today is experiencing a tension between differing models of Church and differing paradigms of evangelization and mission. Although the attempt is being made to resist it, a new model or paradigm is emerging, but it is necessarily emerging from below, not from above. In the long run the tension will be creative. The new model is one that takes human culture seriously, because it envisages a serious dialogue with real human life contexts and patterns of thought. It does not impose a message from above, but elaborates it and lives it from within human societies and cultural traditions. Consequently, it places emphasis on the local, the specific, the 'below'. It is a visibly different kind of Church.

The emerging shape of evangelization

Evangelization is basically the spreading of the Good News about God's Kingdom. It is the revelation of God's saving love, and of his dialogue with humanity – his mission to the world. That mission took a final shape and orientation in the life, death and

resurrection of Jesus Christ, and subsequently in the mandate
which he gave to the Church, which is the seed and the sign of
God's Kingdom. The Church is, therefore, by definition associated
with the divine mission. However, the divine activity goes far
beyond the visible limits of the historical Church in both space
and time. The Kingdom, which Christ fulfilled and which the
Church serves, is an ongoing project of God, whose Spirit is at
work in the hearts of all.

> Thus the Spirit 'who blows where he wills', who was
> already at work in the world before Christ was glorified,
> who 'has filled the world ... holds all things together and
> knows what is said', leads us to broaden our vision so as to
> ponder his activity in every age and place ...
> This is the same Spirit who was at work in the life, death
> and resurrection of Christ and who is at work now in the
> Church.[9]

Spreading the Good News necessarily includes proclamation –
even verbal proclamation, since a name has to be given to the
activity. It is, of course, the name of Jesus Christ, who is
the Saviour, the universal Lord and King. However, proclamation
is secondary to the loving involvement of God with the world,
which is at the origin of the Kingdom. This loving dialogue is
revealed through praxis and prayer, as well as through proclamation. Praxis is focused on community-building and on the preferential option for the poor, who are the special object of God's
attention. Prayer is the living communion of the evangelizer with
God, the divine source of the Kingdom's growth and effectiveness,
and the Christian life of prayer means living under the reign of
God.

It is now possible to see how evangelization has been historically
vitiated by violence and coercion, how it has been subordinated
to materialistic and political motives, flawed by colonial domination and oppression. This has prompted the call for a fresh start,
for a 'new evangelization' that is truly liberative and which really
preaches the Gospel to God's poor. In fact, there is room for 'new
evangelization' in every place and age in order to meet the changing
realities of human cultures and conditions, not least when Christianity is replaced by the secularism of a technological society.
Above all, Christians must beware of the boast that evangelization
is complete. It is not to be equated with Church implanting,
however important that may be, nor with the nominal adherence
to Christianity of a majority of the population. Evangelization is
the ongoing task of the Church and of its members.

Evangelization is essentially a matter of dialogue. In the first place it is a dialogue with human cultures, those patterns of human thought and behaviour which differentiate and identify distinct groups of people. Evangelization does not take place unless it addresses culture and unless it succeeds in bringing about a re-expression of the Gospel and of the Christian life in terms of the culture addressed. This is what has come to be called 'inculturation'. It demands a profound respect for human cultures in their difference, as well as fidelity to the Christ-event and to the outlooks that go back to the New Testament.

In fact, sound theology demands a genuine inculturation of the Good News of the Kingdom. God's creative presence in human cultural traditions invites recognition. It also yearns for a transformation of culture through the mystery of Christ's incarnation, death and resurrection. However, Christ's great commandment of universal love, coupled with his great commission to make disciples of all nations, provides an even clearer theological basis for inculturation. Genuine love must take account of legitimate human differences; it does not seek to abolish them. Evangelization is essentially the love of others in their otherness, otherwise evangelization would constitute a violation of human rights, as happened all too often in the past history of the Church. The human right to an authentic culture implies that evangelizers must recognize a *de facto* equality among cultures, a real liberation of culture. Finally, the theology of the local Church, as the primary ecclesial reality, demands a genuine ongoing dialogue between Gospel and culture, if it is to achieve an identity and autonomy of its own.

Inculturation implies a continuous struggle with syncretism, with the elements of culture which are incompatible with the Gospel. History proves that syncretism is a necessary evil in the Church, and that evangelization is forced to tolerate syncretism up to a point. In fact desyncretization enters into the definition of inculturation itself. What is clear is that fear of syncretism should not be invoked as a reason for postponing inculturation. The cultural patrimony of the Church – the accumulation of diverse cultural elements by the Christian tradition – is itself a syncretic component of inculturation and its contingent character must be acknowledged in practice.

The dialogue with culture usually involves a dialogue with other faiths. Advancing the reign of God, or spreading his Kingdom, necessarily entails working with God's Spirit in the world towards a final consummation in Christ that transcends the historical Church we now know, as well as the other faith traditions. The Church needs to develop and grow. Inter-faith dialogue is strictly necessary for the salvation of the Church and for God's ongoing self-revelation in the Church. That is why an encounter has to take place with other religions, and why evangelizers need to reflect upon what is of God in the other faiths which they encounter and to which they also testify in faith. The aim of dialogue is definitely not to annex other faiths, nor is it merely a strategy for more effective evangelization. It is simply an integral part of the evangelization process, which itself is oriented towards God's loving dialogue with humanity.

Dialogue is primarily a dialogue of life and action, rather than a sharing in worship or theological discussion. It is an informal, rather than an institutional, type of dialogue, an interpersonal sharing of lived faith.

Evangelization is not only culturally liberative, but is directed towards a comprehensive liberation of humanity. Such a liberation is the outcome of the Kingdom. God's reign sets people free – in the first place, from sin and evil, both personal and social. Evangelization opens people's eyes to the oppression and injustice caused by sin, and helps bring social reality into line with the Gospel ideal. This leads to socio-economic liberation and the reaffirmation of human rights and freedoms. One of the most effective evangelizing instruments where liberation is concerned has been the basic ecclesial community, as developed in Latin America, Africa and the Far East. Such communities provide the classic instance of the rich and powerful being evangelized by the poor. They promote the kind of solidarity and neighbourliness that instances God's dialogue of love with the world. However, they also point to a perfection of liberation when the Kingdom is finally revealed.

Evangelization and the ecclesial paradigm shift

Baptism and confirmation make us all evangelizers. If the Church is really serious about evangelization, then we should not merely be initiated into the Christian spiritual life, we should also be initiated into the work of evangelization itself. We should not be content to become passive 'consumers' of Christianity, but active promoters of the faith. The Church especially needs young evangelizers.

As evangelizers we do not act alone. On the contrary, we are baptized into a community of faith and we belong to a local Church, through our ties of family and neighbourhood. This is made clearer still where basic ecclesial communities are active and where they articulate the reality that is 'Church'. Religious communities are also privileged instruments of evangelization. In fact, it is true to say that evangelization typically possesses a community dimension.

The contemplative vocation is one of withdrawal from the world, but it is a withdrawal which takes place within, and on behalf of, the local community. Through the communion of saints, it helps to achieve the goals of evangelization. The Holy Spirit renders the work of contemplation effective in realizing the Kingdom. Prayer is inseparable from evangelization, and the contemplative vocation is both a sign of its importance to the evangelizer and a supplement to it. Contemplative evangelization is also carried out through direct forms of visible witness, chiefly in charity towards the poor and disadvantaged.

Pastoral evangelization is the ordinary, active form of spreading God's Kingdom. It operates within the sphere of a reasonably homogeneous and integrated community. It is concerned with the extensive and intensive growth of this community and with the living of the Gospel in its real life contexts. Liturgical prayer is basic to this form of evangelization. It helps people discover and respond to Christ in their lives. Consequently, it requires constant reflection and social analysis, if pastoral workers are to respond continuously to changing human life contexts. They need to identify those which are unevangelized but which are potentially receptive to the Good News. Christians are called to demonstrate that their faith is far from being a purely private affair, and that it is relevant to many areas of modern life. Dialogue with these various 'worlds' is therefore a major concern of pastoral evangelization. They include the secular ethos, politics, the media, women and youth subcultures, ecumenism and new religious movements and cults.

Pastoral evangelization is not merely a holding operation. On the contrary, it is a commitment to continuous conversion, and even to what might be called a refounding of the Church. Pastors are part of the people of God, and pastoral evangelization is essentially a work of partnership between Christians at every level in the community.

Missionary evangelization occurs when the evangelizer leaves his or her home community and crosses a human frontier to help spread the Kingdom of God in another culture. We cannot ultimately eliminate cultural and language barriers, even if we wanted to, and, even with a world technocracy controlled by the West, the idea of universal culture remains a fantasy – perhaps a nightmare. Frontiers, however, can be crossed, whether they are geographical, psychological, or socio-cultural. The complexity of mission contexts today is brought about by the increase of population mobility and the multicultural character of many countries. It is not always necessary to travel a great distance in order to be a missionary evangelizer. Although primary evangelization is usually a priority for missionaries, it does not define missionary evangelization. What defines it is the act of crossing a cultural frontier, whatever evangelizing activities are carried out.

The Catholic Church today – as we saw earlier in this chapter – is experiencing a paradigm shift in mission. There are those who cling to an outmoded paradigm and would gladly restore it. This is the old Eurocentric model of mission, in which the Western Church is credited with stability and maturity, and with the right to send missionaries to the 'pagan' nations of the non-Western world. Such new Churches are to remain indefinitely under the tutelage of the Christian West. In this paradigm, missionaries are sent by centralized organizations on behalf of the universal Church.

This paradigm has been forced to come to terms with the changed missionary realities of the present day, with the recognition of cultural pluralism and equality, with the abolition of the *ius commissionis* and the reinstatement (at least in theory) of the local Church, and with the weakened state of the old, Western, mission-sending Church. Those who would restore the old paradigm of mission cannot in fact put the clock back, and are forced to confront the anomalies which have arisen, however reluctant they may be to accept change.[10]

The build-up of these anomalies indicates that a new mission paradigm is emerging. It is the paradigm of the *koinonia* Church in which a mutual ministry is taking place among local Churches, which are all mission-sending, and which are reaching out to one another in their various needs. There is a growing partnership and mutual respect among these local Churches which is verified by the present pattern of missionary recruitment. Mission in this paradigm is essentially dialogical, encountering other cultures and faiths. It is also typified by the witness of basic ecclesial communities. Above all, there is a consciousness of the need to give creative expression to Christianity in accordance with the evangelized cultures. It is the image of an egalitarian world communion of local Churches, enriching one another – a communion guaranteed and served by the central organs of the universal Church.

Under the new paradigm of mission the missionary evangelizer needs a specialist formation. This is a professional training which equips him or her to cross cultural frontiers, and includes social and cultural anthropology. Lectures in this subject must be supplemented by an 'immersion' experience, a real research contact with a mission context which can be integrated with the study programme.

Primary evangelization is obviously a priority before Church implantation has taken place, but it may equally remain a priority after the local Church has been founded and has become viable. Ecclesial maturity is not to be simply equated with the absence of missionaries. Today, the need for foreign missionaries can be dictated by many new factors, not least the phenomenon of population mobility, but missionaries are required to phase into the local Church where they work.

It would seem that – in the spirit of the new missionary paradigm – primary evangelization applies to the secularized post-Christian Western world, especially where a majority of people have no Christian faith. In such situations it does not seem helpful to appeal to the 'Christian' character of their culture. Culture belongs to a people and does not have some kind of impersonal existence. On the contrary, modern, post-Christian culture is frequently subversive of the Gospel and its values. The great challenge to the evangelizer does not consist in helping Western men and women to overcome their indifference to a past Christian culture, but in countering the dehumanizing and dechristianizing effects of a modern, technological culture.

Countering restorationism in the Church

The most serious obstacles to evangelization arise from within the Church. This is especially true where inculturation is concerned. The chief obstacle is the wilful refusal to distinguish between unity and uniformity. What is needed is a commitment to pluriformity, to a Church that is culturally polycentric. This is demanded by the nature of inculturation itself, which can only come from below. Obstruction of inculturation from above could lead to an outward conformity that conceals a far-reaching internal heterodoxy, or at best could drive inculturation underground.

Failure to implement inculturation in practice implies an alliance with the secular Europeanization of the world and a failure to uphold the religious values of indigenous cultures. However, there are those who believe in the essentially Christian character of Western culture and in its providential role for uniting a world Church. Such a view spells disaster for evangelization. More often the assumption is made that the Gospel, or even the Church, exists in some culture-free form. There is talk about the 'essence of the Gospel' and about culture as an extrinsic, separable reality. Or else emphasis is placed on the Gospel challenging and transforming culture, rather than on culture re-expressing the Gospel. The

Church is even envisaged as a culture in its own right. Frequently, in official statements, the need is expressed for an exaggerated slowness in carrying out inculturation, in order to lessen the supposed risk of syncretism, although, at other times, the urgency of inculturation is also stressed. Clearly, inculturation is largely regarded as, at best, a remote prospect.

In the end, the issue cannot be sidestepped. 'Inculturation is diversification.'[11] In practice, this means entrusting the responsibility for inculturation to the national episcopal conference, since dioceses can seldom be identified with a culture or cluster of cultures, and the Second Vatican Council referred, in this context, to the 'major socio-cultural region'.[12] Evangelization, properly understood, can help indigenous peoples to redefine their cultures in the face of Western cultural aggression. This, in turn, requires a new model of Church – a culturally polycentric Church.

'Refounding' the Church

An evangelizing Church must implement the great commandment which is the source and first impulse of evangelization, the commandment of universal, fraternal love. This commandment stems from the nature of God himself and of his mission to humanity. It is is the basic characteristic of the Kingdom which the Church proclaims and to which it is called to conform. This commandment of love precludes any desire to impose alien cultural traditions upon people or to violate their right to culture. On the contrary, it invites the evangelizer to penetrate other cultural traditions and to identify with them.

The Church needs to be healed, even refounded, in the light of this original commandment of Christ, if its evangelization is to become effective. It must become a more obvious sign of the Kingdom. To do this it needs to purge everything which is at variance with the Gospel: judgemental attitudes, condemnations, intimidation, manipulation and subterfuge. Authority needs to be exercised with mercy, openness and love, attitudes inviting solidarity and co-responsibility, not the victimization or stigmatization of inferiors.

The Church needs to be 'refounded', in the sense given to that word by Gerald Arbuckle.[13] This is not a question of abolishing institutions and structures, but a reshaping of them, a change of method, a spiritual renewal and a return to the original source in Jesus Christ, the Word of God. It also implies the wholehearted acceptance of the emerging paradigm of mission, and the adoption of a new Church model. The Church has traditionally operated with a number of models, which have been given varied emphasis at different times. The model which best fits the needs of evangelization is that of the *koinonia* Church. It is a model in which the experience of community is basic and in which visible, cultural differences are legitimated. It is also a model which opposes the socio-economic hegemony of the West and which resists the temptation of manipulating economically dependent local Churches. In the *koinonia* Church there are as many cultural centres as there are viable local cultures.

The study of the Christian communities in the New Testament reveals that the formulation of faith is subject to progressive development and to a plurality of expression. A culturally polycentric Church needs to be more tolerant of theological pluriformity. The Pope would work more closely with the world's bishops and delegate much of his ordinary teaching to them. The Petrine primacy would then be exercised in a context of collegiality, rather than the Pope being the virtual mouthpiece of the bishops. From the point of view of evangelization, this would be much more effective.

The very concept of theology will become pluriform in such a Church, but there will be mechanisms for bridging the different approaches and a theological commission which can operate a cross-cultural hermeneutic in order to facilitate the mutual theological enrichment of local Churches. The 1983 Code of Canon Law, which reflects the moribund paradigm, needs to be scaled down to provide a framework within which local Churches can formulate their own legislative codes. From being the greatest single obstacle to inculturation, Canon Law should become a source of confidence and creativity in the local Churches. Fully developed structures should enable local Churches to take full advantage of the law. Greater provision should be made for the holding of deliberative councils at regional levels.

There is no sense in making an artificial break with immediate liturgical traditions, but local Churches should be encouraged to develop their own liturgical rites in directions unforeseen by centralized authority and for which no models necessarily exist. New liturgies should grow organically from the old. However, special liturgical regions of the Roman rite should be created within which bishops can take their own decisions, without the need for explicit central approval in every instance.

The Pope's ministry would also be exercised in the context of the new model. His service to Catholicity would be to sanction cultural pluriformity in the Church, to confirm the faith of local Churches, offer them leadership and guidance – principally through their own bishops – and to operate a process of mutual enrichment among the local Churches. The emphasis should be on empowering others, not on centralized approval or disapproval.

Basic community as a guarantee for the future

At present, there are few signs that the Catholic leadership is ready to adopt the *koinonia* Church model, or even that it accepts the reality of the new missionary paradigm. When it eventually does so, the Church will be a better instrument for evangelization, if indeed it is not too late. In the meantime the flame is being carried and kept alight by the basic communities Church. With their freedom and spontaneity, basic ecclesial communities are best fitted to carry out an authentic evangelization from below.

Evangelization is most effective when it operates through interpersonal relationships and through the charity and concern of Christian neighbourliness. The basic Christian community encourages and practises good neighbourliness in its care for those in need, and in its practical pursuit of justice and peace. It is a cell of committed Christians at the service of the Church which comprises all the integral elements of evangelization: inculturation, liberation and dialogue. It evangelizes the local culture, as well as those who adhere to this culture. At a popular level, it carries out an ongoing dialogue with human cultures, traditions and religions. The basic Christian community strives to rekindle the flame of faith in the neighbourhood. It is committed to the restoration of social and personal morality and it tries to make its own small contribution to liberation from injustice and the abuse of human rights.

Although they are ecclesial, basic Christian communities enjoy a structural freedom which is opposed to totalitarianism, and which benefits evangelization, because they can produce initiatives which emerge from the actual life context of Christians. The fact that they are also instruments of the pastoral team contributes to this effectiveness. They are also instances of collaborative ministry, bringing together the sexes and different conditions and classes of people in a manner that is not possible at other levels of the Church. This collaboration of men and women in the evangelizing tasks of the basic Christian community offers a powerful witness, which may well be prophetic for the whole Church. It exemplifies the very meaning of Catholicity and the service of the Kingdom.

The communities-based local Church is a worshipping Church and a Scripture-reading Church. It is also a caring Church which offers its service of evangelization to the Holy Spirit at work in the world, for the building of God's Kingdom. The communities-based Church is the best guarantee of the emergent missionary paradigm, with its emphasis on the local and the 'below'. It augurs well for a culturally polycentric Church.

Our examination of evangelization, therefore, has first of all confronted us with the nature of God's Kingdom and the way in which it is built up through proclamation, praxis and prayer. It has led us on to a consideration of the integral elements of evangelization: inculturation, dialogue and liberation. We have then seen how evangelization is articulated through the three basic forms of the Christian vocation: the contemplative, the pastoral and the missionary. This has led us to consider the paradigm shift in mission and the various obstacles within and outside the Church to the emergence of this paradigm. Finally, we have drawn the ecclesiological conclusion – the need for a *koinonia* Church, and the role of basic ecclesial communities in paving the way for this new Church model.

References

1 Andrew Hake, *African Metropolis: Nairobi's Self-Help City* (London: University of Sussex Press, 1977).
2 Aylward Shorter, *Toward a Theology of Inculturation* (London: Geoffrey Chapman/Maryknoll, NY: Orbis Books, 1988), pp. 251ff.
3 This is not his real name.
4 Louise Pirouet, 'A Comparison of the Responses of Three Societies to Christianity', mimeographed paper presented to the University Social Sciences Council Conference, Kampala, 1969.
5 Cf. Aylward Shorter, *The Church in the African City* (London: Geoffrey Chapman/Maryknoll, NY: Orbis Books, 1991).
6 *Instrumentum Laboris*, 89.
7 *Redemptoris Missio*, 8.
8 *Lumen Gentium*, 23.
9 *Redemptoris Missio*, 29.
10 In Chapter 3 we argued that the missionary encyclical *Redemptoris Missio* was a product of the creative tension between old and new paradigms.
11 J.-Y. Calvez, 'The Real Problems of Inculturation', *Lumen Vitae*, vol. 40, no. 1 (1985), p. 73.
12 *Ad Gentes Divinitus*, 22.
13 Gerald A. Arbuckle, *Earthing the Gospel* (London: Geoffrey Chapman/Maryknoll, NY: Orbis Books, 1990), pp. 208–20.

Index

Index